COGAT®
GRADE 1
VERBAL

3 Practice Tests
Level 7

Savant Test Prep™

www.SavantPrep.com

Please leave a review for this book!

Thank you for purchasing this resource.

Please take a moment to leave a
review on the website where you purchased this.

TABLE OF CONTENTS

INTRODUCTION

COGAT® GENERAL INFORMATION

- COGAT® stands for Cognitive Abilities Test®.
- The test measures students' reasoning skills and problem-solving skills.
- It provides educators with an overall assessment of students' academic strengths and weaknesses.
- The COGAT® is commonly used as a screener for gifted and talented programs.
    - Gifted and Talented (G&T) selection sometimes requires a teacher recommendation as well.
- The test is usually administered in a group setting.
- A teacher (or other school associate) administers the test, reading the directions.
- Please check with your school/testing site regarding its testing procedures, as these may differ.

COGAT® LEVEL 7 FORMAT

- Students in first grade take the COGAT® Level 7.
- The Verbal Battery has 48 questions.
- The test is divided into 3 main parts, each called a "Battery." Each Battery has three question types. See the chart below.

VERBAL BATTERY	NON-VERBAL BATTERY	QUANTITATIVE BATTERY
Picture Analogies: 16 Questions	Figure Analogies: 16 Questions	Number Puzzles: 12 Questions
Picture Classification: 16 Questions	Figure Classification: 16 Questions	Number Series: 16 Questions
Sentence Completion: 16 Questions	Paper Folding: 12 Questions	Number Analogies: 16 Questions

- Often, schools administer one Battery per day, allowing approximately 45 minutes per Battery.
- Students have around 15 minutes to complete each question type (for example, students would have around 15 minutes to complete Picture Analogies).
- See the following pages for examples and explanations of each question type.

COGAT® SCORING

- Students receive points for correct answers. Points are not deducted for incorrect answers. (Therefore, students should at least guess versus leaving a question blank.)
- In general, schools have a "cut-off" COGAT® score, which they consider together with additional criteria, for gifted & talented acceptance. This varies by school.
- This score is usually at least 98%. (However, some schools accept scores of 95% or even 85%.)
- A score of 98% means that your child scored as well as, or better than, 98% of those in his/her testing group.
- COGAT® scores are available for the entire test and can be broken down by Battery.
- Depending on the school/program, such a "cut-off" score may only be required on one or two of the Batteries (and not on the test overall).
- It is essential to check with your school/program for their acceptance procedures.
- The COGAT® Practice Tests in this book can not yield these percentiles because they have not been given to a large enough group of students to produce an accurate comparison/calculation.

HOW TO USE THIS BOOK

1. Go over the Question Examples together with your child. These begin on the next page.

2. Do Practice Test 1 (Workbook Format)
   - Do these questions with your child, especially if this is your child's first exposure to COGAT®-prep questions. These questions have a "workbook format," meaning they are meant to be done together.
   - Do not assign a time limit.
   - Talk about what the question is asking your child to do.
   - Questions progress in difficulty. (The first few questions are quite simple.)
   - Go over the answers using the Answer Key.
   - For questions missed, go over the answers again, discussing what makes the correct answer better than the other choices.

3. Do the remaining Practice Tests following Practice Test 1.
   - If your child progressed easily through Practice Test 1, see how well they can do without your help.
   - If your child needed assistance with much of Practice Test 1, then continue to assist your child with Practice Test 2.
   - If you wish to assign a time limit, assign around 15 minutes per question type.
   - Go over the answers using the Answer Key.
   - For questions missed, go over the answers again, discussing what makes the correct answer better than the other choices.

4. **Need more practice?**

   - **Help your child ace the test!**

   - **Check out Savant Test Prep™ books on Amazon®.**

TEST-TAKING TIPS

- Ensure your child listens carefully to the directions.
- Make sure (s)he does not rush through questions. (There is no prize for finishing first!) Tell your child to look carefully at the question. Then, tell your child to look at each answer choice before marking his/her answer.
    - If you notice your child continuing to rush through the questions, tell him/her to point to each part of the question. Then, point to each answer choice.
- If (s)he does not know the answer, then use the process of elimination. Cross out any answer choices which are clearly incorrect, then choose from those remaining.
- This tip/suggestion is entirely at your discretion. You may wish to offer some sort of special motivation to encourage your child to do his/her best. An extra incentive of, for example, an art set, a building block set, or a special outing can go a long way in motivating young learners!
- The night before testing, make sure your child has enough sleep, without any interruptions. (Think about the difference in **your** brain function with a good night's sleep vs. without. The same goes for your child's.)
- The morning before the test, ensure your child eats a healthy breakfast with protein and complex carbs. Do not let them eat sugar, chocolate, etc.
- If you can choose the time your child will take the test (for example, if (s)he will take the test individually, instead of at school with a group), opt for a morning testing session, when your child will be most alert.

QUESTION EXAMPLES

- Here is an overview of the COGAT® question types.
- This section has examples to introduce your child to test concepts.
  - Do these together with your child.
- Below the questions are explanations for parents.

1. PICTURE ANALOGIES (VERBAL BATTERY)

- **Directions (read to child):** The pictures in the top boxes go together in some way. Look at the bottom boxes. One box is empty. Look at the row of pictures next to the boxes. These are the answer choices. Which one of these choices goes with the picture in the bottom box like the pictures in the top boxes go together?

- **Explanation (for parents):** Your child must figure out how the images in the top set of boxes are related and belong together. Then, (s)he must figure out which answer choice would go with the bottom left image so that the bottom set would have the same analogous relationship as the top set. (The small arrows demonstrate that the images go together.)

- **Strategy 1:** Define a "rule" to describe how the top set belongs together. Then, take this "rule" and use it with the bottom picture. Look at the answer choices, and figure out which answer would make the bottom set follow your "rule."

- **Using the above question as an example, say to your child:**
In this question, we see a spider and a web. A spider's home is its web. A rule would be, "the thing in the first box has as its home the thing in the second box." On the bottom, we see a bird. Let's try the answer choices with our rule. A flower is not correct because a bird's home is not a flower, nor is a bench or another bird. A nest is correct because it's a bird's home.

- **Strategy 2:** Try to come up with a sentence to describe how the top set belongs together. Then, use this sentence with the bottom picture. Look at the answer choices, and figure out which answer would make the sentence work with this bottom set. With both strategies, if more than one answer choice works, then you need a more specific rule/sentence.

- The examples on the next page outline some of the logic used in analogy questions. While the COGAT® uses pictures (not words) at this level in verbal analogies, this will still help familiarize your child with analogy logic.

• Directions (read to child): I am going to read you a question. The words go together in some way. One word is missing. Next, I will read you the answer choices. Let's figure out which one is the missing word.
(Parent note: the answer and logic are below the question.)

Question	Answer Choices			
1. Spider -is to- Web as Bird -is to- ? *Answer - Nest (Animal: Animal's Home)*	Flower	Bench	Nest	Bird
2. Acorns -are to- Squirrel as Seeds -are to- ? *Answer - Bird (Animal: Animal's Food)*	Grass	Bird	Fish	Snake
3. Calf -is to- Cow as Cub -is to- ? *Answer - Tiger (Animal Baby: Animal Adult)*	Tiger	Horse	Goose	Bull
4. Lion -is to- Fur as Snake -is to- ? *Answer - Scales (Animal: Animal's Covering)*	Lizard	Hair	Fangs	Scales
5. Happy -is to- Sad as Wet -is to- ? *Answer - Dry (Opposites)*	Damp	Clean	Water	Dry
6. Tiger -is to- Cheetah as Butterfly -is to- ? *Answer - Moth (Similar: Similar (Flying Insects))*	Bird	Bat	Moth	Jaguar
7. Flower -is to- Bouquet as Kernel -is to- ? *Answer - Corn Cob (Part: Whole)*	Snack	Plant	Corn Cob	Crop
8. Ship -is to- Port as Car -is to- ? *Answer - Garage (Object: Location)*	Truck	Garage	Marina	Wheel
9. Pencil -is to- Paper as Paint -is to- ? *Answer - Wall (Object: Object Used With)*	Wall	Color	Red	Light
10. Lumber -is to- Fence as Paper -is to- ? *Answer - Book (Object: Product That Object Is Put Together To Make)*	Log	Branch	Tree	Book
11. Cheese -is to- Refrigerator as Ice -is to- ? *Answer - Freezer (Object: Item Used to Store/Hold Object)*	Snow	Toaster	Freezer	Cube
12. Box -is to- Cube as Globe -is to- ? *Answer - Sphere (Object: Similar Shape)*	Prism	Sphere	Oval	Pentagon
13. Straw -is to- Juice as Spoon -is to- ? *Answer - Cereal (Utensil: Object Utensil Is Used With)*	Cereal	Salad	Steak	Sandwich
14. Egg -is to- Chicken as Milk -is to- ? *Answer - Cow (Food/Drink: Source of Food/Drink)*	Chick	Cheese	Rooster	Cow
15. Ambulance -is to- Paramedic as Tractor -is to- ? *Answer - Farmer (Vehicle: User)*	Doctor	Teacher	Scientist	Farmer
16. Doctor -is to- Stethoscope as Carpenter -is to- ? *Answer - Hammer (Worker Who Uses Object: Object)*	Boot	Builder	Cabinet	Hammer

2. PICTURE CLASSIFICATION (VERBAL BATTERY)

• **Directions (read to child):** The top row shows three pictures that are alike in some way. Look at the bottom row. There are four pictures. Which picture in the bottom row goes best with the pictures in the top row?

• **Explanation (for parents):** Together with your child, try to figure out a "rule" describing how the top pictures are alike and belong together. Then, apply the "rule" to each answer choice to determine which one follows it. If your child finds that more than one choice follows the rule, then a more specific rule is needed.

• **Using the above question as an example, say to your child:** In the top row, we see a ladybug, a party hat, and a dog. What do these have in common? It may be hard to see at first. Let's have another look. Each of these has spots. This is how they are alike. The only answer choice that has spots is the cheetah.

• **Tip:** You can help your child improve classification using items you see in everyday life or in books.

• The classification examples on the next page outline some of the logic used in classification questions. While the COGAT® uses pictures (not words) at this level in verbal analogies, this will still help familiarize your child with classification logic.

• **Directions (read to child):** I am going to read you a group of words. The words go together in some way. Let's figure out how the words go together. Then, I will read you another group of words. Let's figure out which one from this group goes best with the words in the first group.

(Parent note: the answer and logic are below the question.)

Question				Answer Choices			
1. Cave	Hive	Web		Spider	Nest	Vet	Bat

Answer - Nest (Animal Homes)

2. Butterfly	Ant	Bee		Worm	Horse	Bird	Dragonfly

Answer - Dragonfly (Animal Types (Insects))

3. Forest	Jungle	Desert		Tree	Valley	Rainforest	City

Answer - Rainforest (Habitats)

4. Lemon	Grape	Apple		Strawberry	Farm	Sweet	Lettuce

Answer - Strawberry (Kinds of Food (Fruit))

5. Scientist	Nurse	Detective		Superhero	Teenager	Pilot	Fairy

Answer - Pilot (Jobs)

6. Sock	Skate	Boot		Slipper	Cap	Mitten	Toe

Answer - Slipper (Objects Worn On Feet)

7. Hot Air Balloon	Jet	Helicopter		Ship	Airport	Bird	Airplane

Answer - Airplane (Vehicles for Air Travel)

8. Ruler	Measuring Tape	Scale		Thermometer	TV	Pen	Number

Answer - Thermometer (Object Use (Used to Measure))

9. Pillow	Blanket	Mattress		Towel	Chair	Sheet	Table

Answer - Sheet (Object Location (Found on Beds))

10. Fire	Sun	Stove		Cookie	Toaster	Beach	Camp

Answer - Toaster (Object Characteristics (Provide Heat))

11. Planet	Ball	Globe		Country	Goal	Bubble	Racetrack

Answer - Bubble (Object Shape (Spherical))

3. SENTENCE COMPLETION (VERBAL BATTERY)

• **Directions (read to child):** Listen to the question, then choose the best answer.

Which one of these shows a pair?

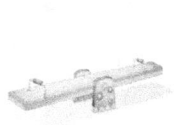   

• **Explanation (for parents):** Unlike Picture Analogies and Picture Classification, Sentence Completion questions have different directions. The above example is a very simple one. (The answer is C.) The questions in this book's two practice tests will be more challenging.

• Make sure your child listens carefully to these questions. Test administrators will not repeat the questions.

• If listening is challenging for your child, tell him/her to repeat the directions back to you. Remind your child to listen to the entire question. (Some children will stop listening if they think they already know the answer.)

• Tell him/her to pay special attention to "negative" words like "not" or "no." (The two practice tests include questions like this.)

Practice Test 1 (Workbook Format) begins on the next page.

Parents, read the below with your child.

Watch out!

This book is filled with tricky questions. Can you answer them?

Of course you can!

Pay close attention to each question and try your best.

We'll be here to help you along the way!

10

COGAT® PRACTICE TEST 1
(WORKBOOK FORMAT)

PICTURE ANALOGIES

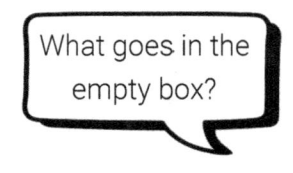

Sara

Directions (read to child): The pictures in the top boxes go together in some way. One box on the bottom is empty. Look at the row of pictures next to the boxes. These are the answer choices. Which one of these goes with the picture in the bottom box like the pictures in the top boxes go together?

Explanation (for parents): A more detailed explanation and example questions are on p. 6-7. If you have not already, look these over. Following is an excerpt.

Your child must figure out how the images in the top set of boxes are related and belong together. Then, (s)he must figure out which answer choice would go with the bottom left image so that the bottom set would have the same analogous relationship as the top set. (The small arrows demonstrate that the images go together.)

Example (read this to child): Look at the boxes on top. In the first box, we see a hand. In the second box, we see a mitten. (Together, try to come up with a "rule" describing how they are alike and go together.) A hand goes inside a mitten. The object in the second box is what is worn on the object in the first box. Let's look in the bottom box. We see a foot. Now, let's look at the answer choices. Which one goes with the picture of a foot in the same way that the pictures in the top row go together? The sock (the second choice). A sock is worn on a foot.

Parent note: A common mistake for kids would be picking an answer that simply "has to do with" the first box. There is more than one answer choice that "has to do with" a foot. A sock and a footprint both have to do a foot. A footprint (choice D) does not follow the rule, and it does not have the same relationship. A sock (choice C) follows the rule. Also, watch out for answer choices that have to do with objects on the top row. For example, a scarf and a hat have to do with a mitten, but they do not follow the rule either.

1.

2.

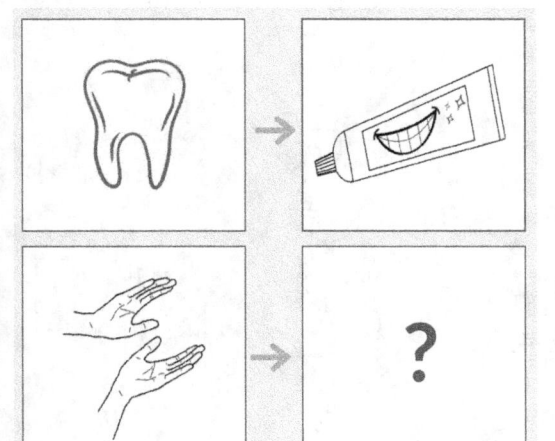

(A)

(B)

(C)

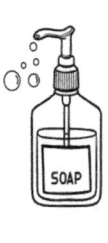

(D)

3.

(A)

(B)

(C)

(D)

4.

(A)

(B)

(C)

(D)

5.

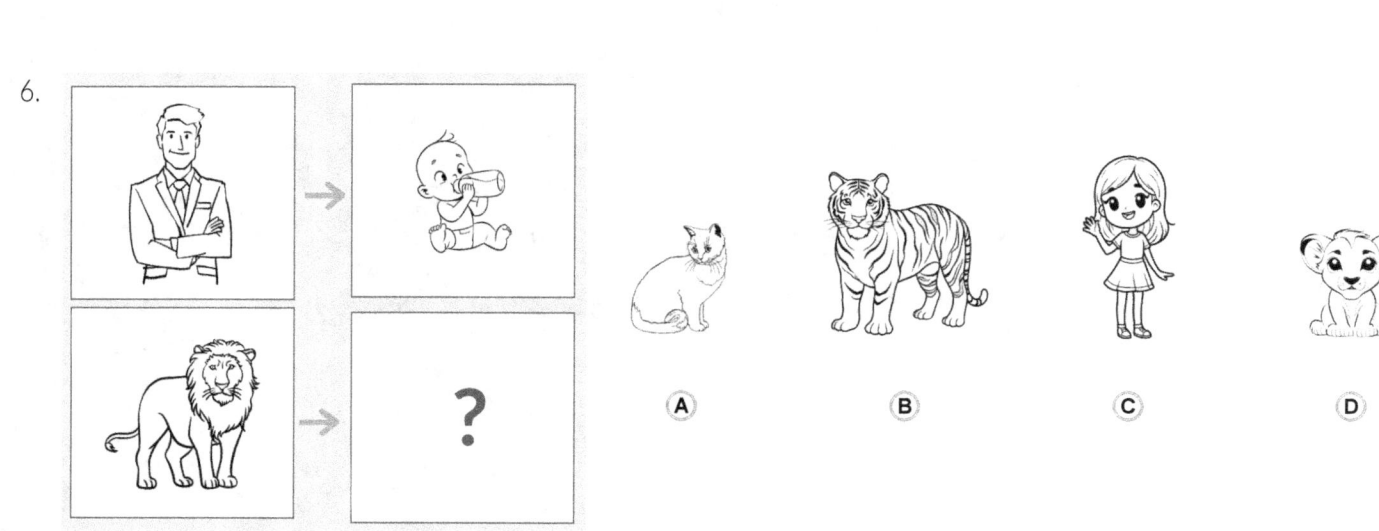

A   B   C   D

6.

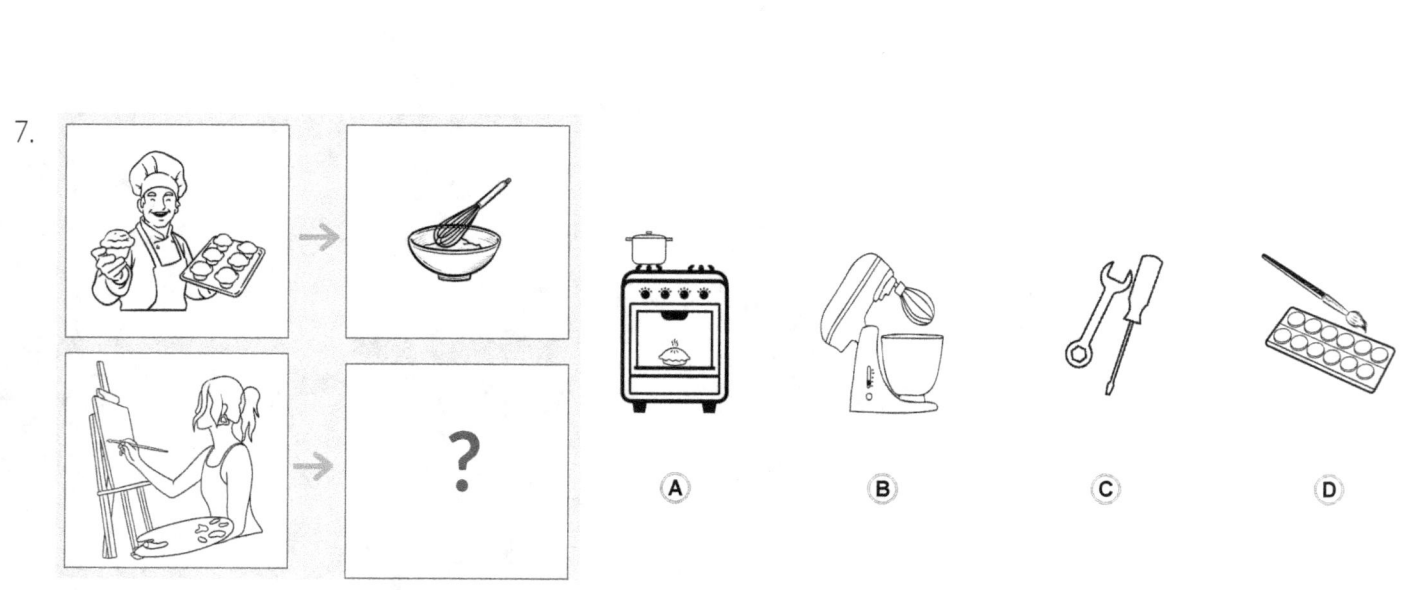

A   B   C   D

7.

14

8.

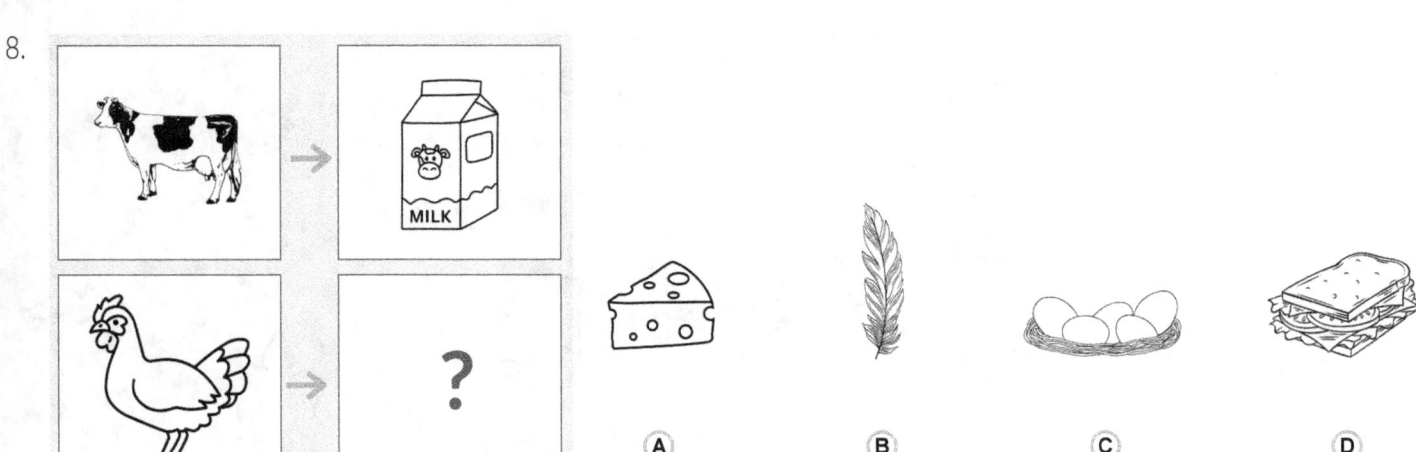

A   B   C   D

9.

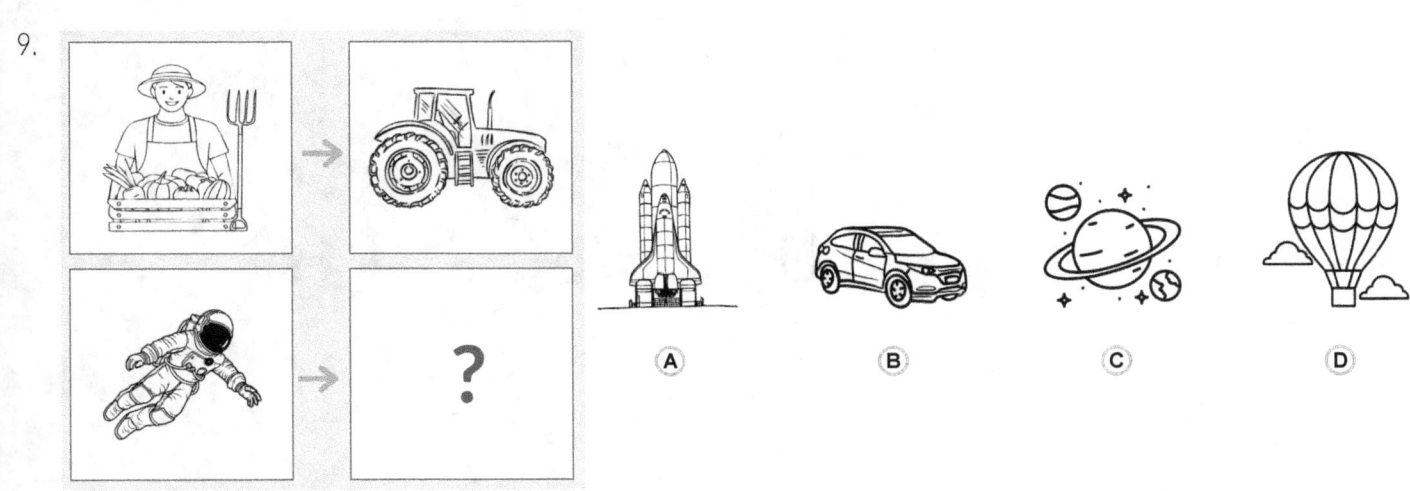

A   B   C   D

10.

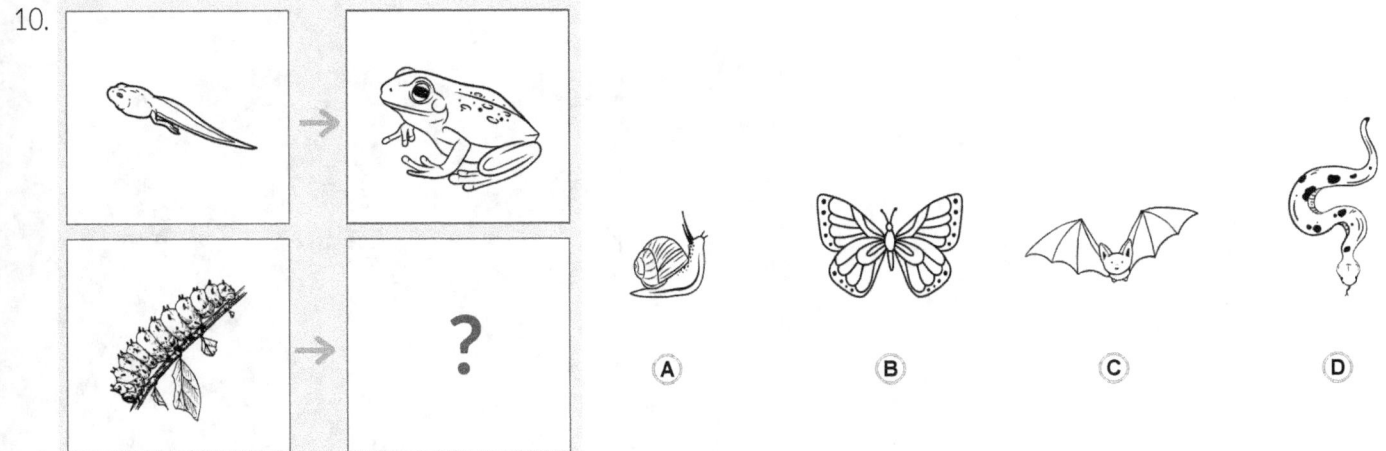

A   B   C   D

15

11.

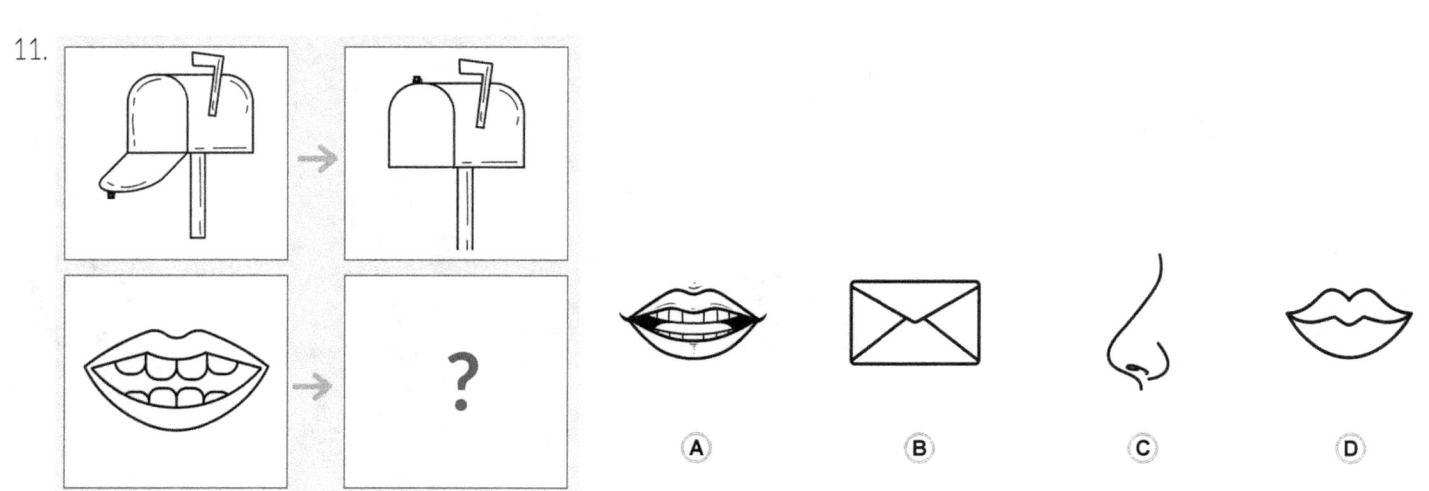

12.

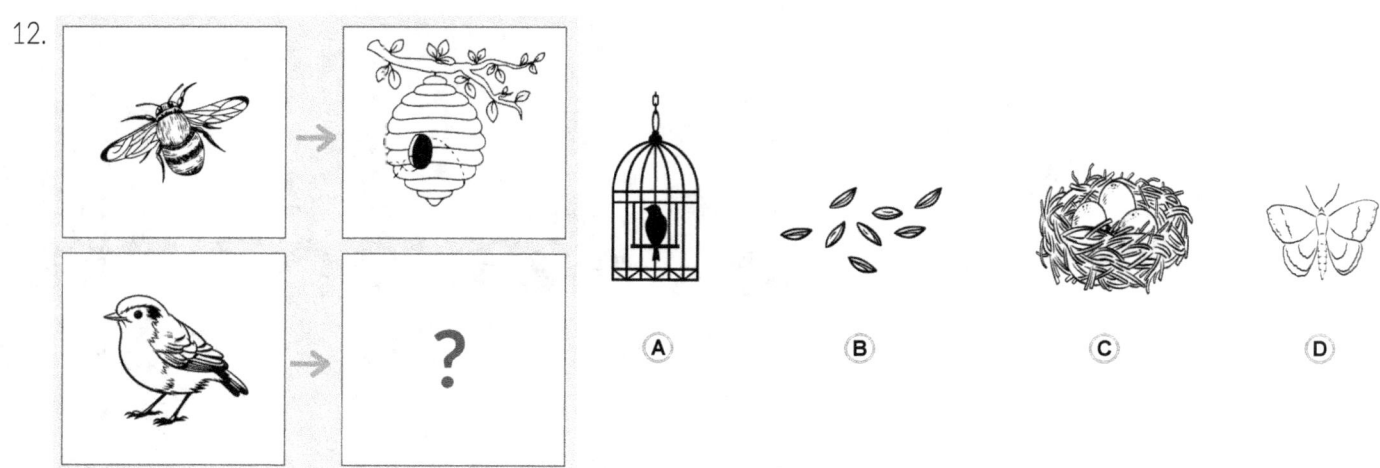

13.

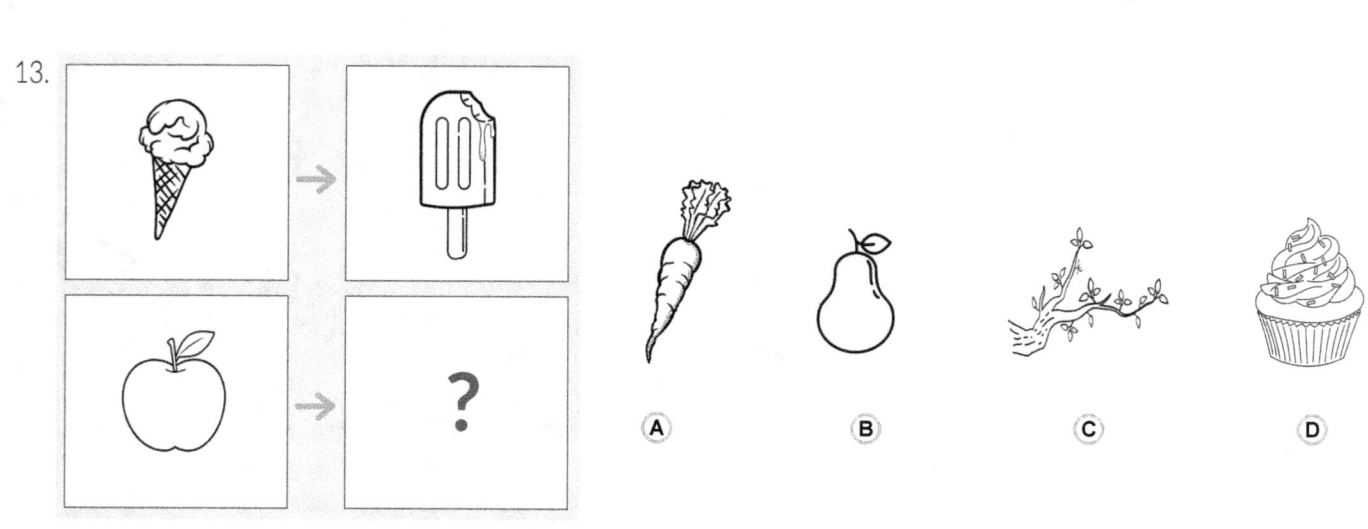

14.

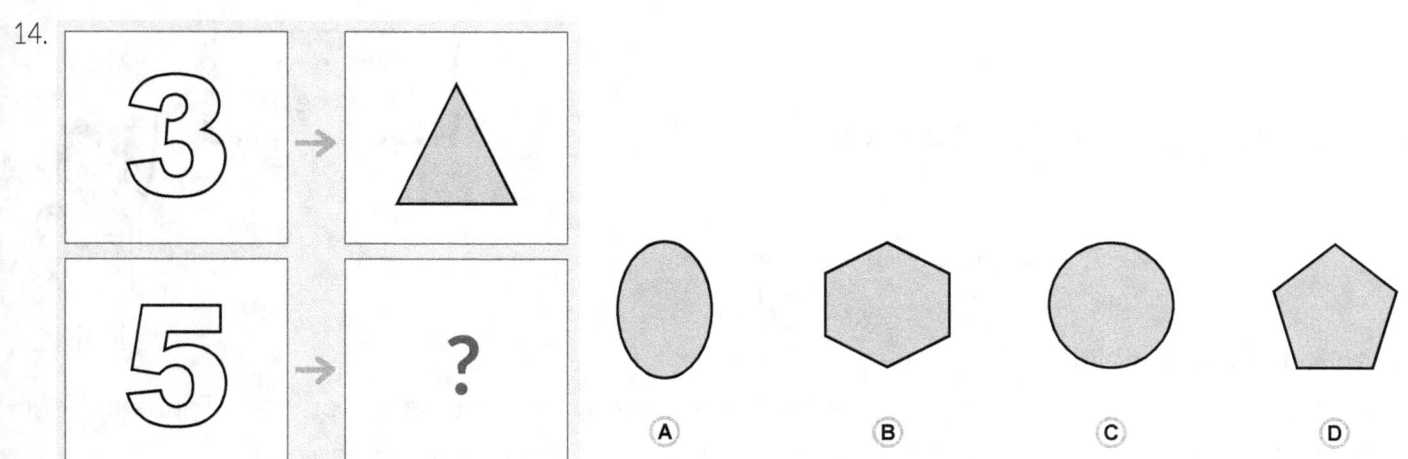

15.

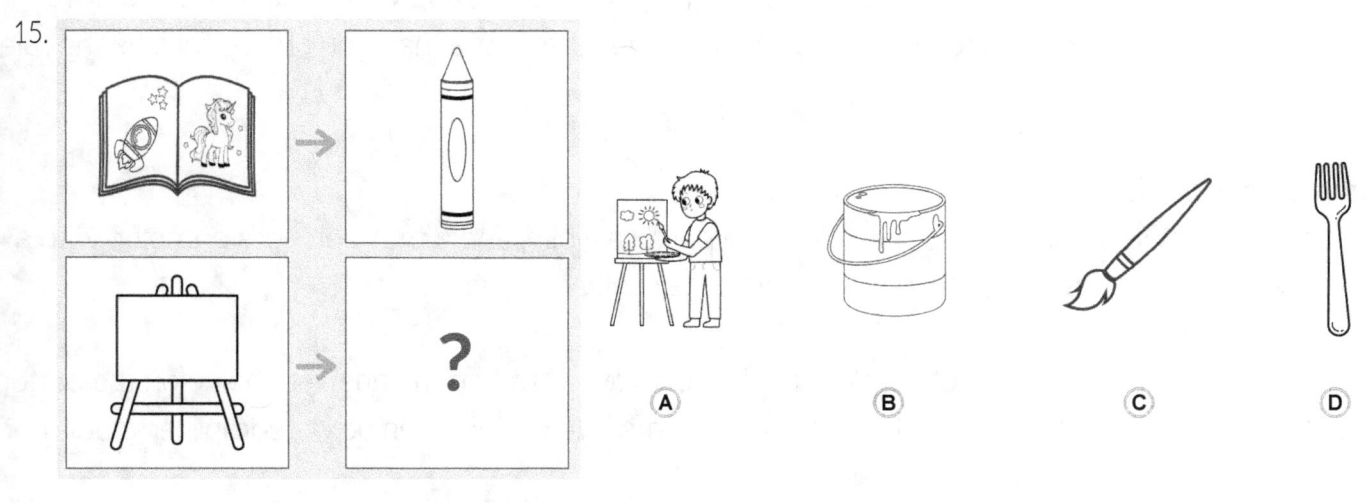

16.

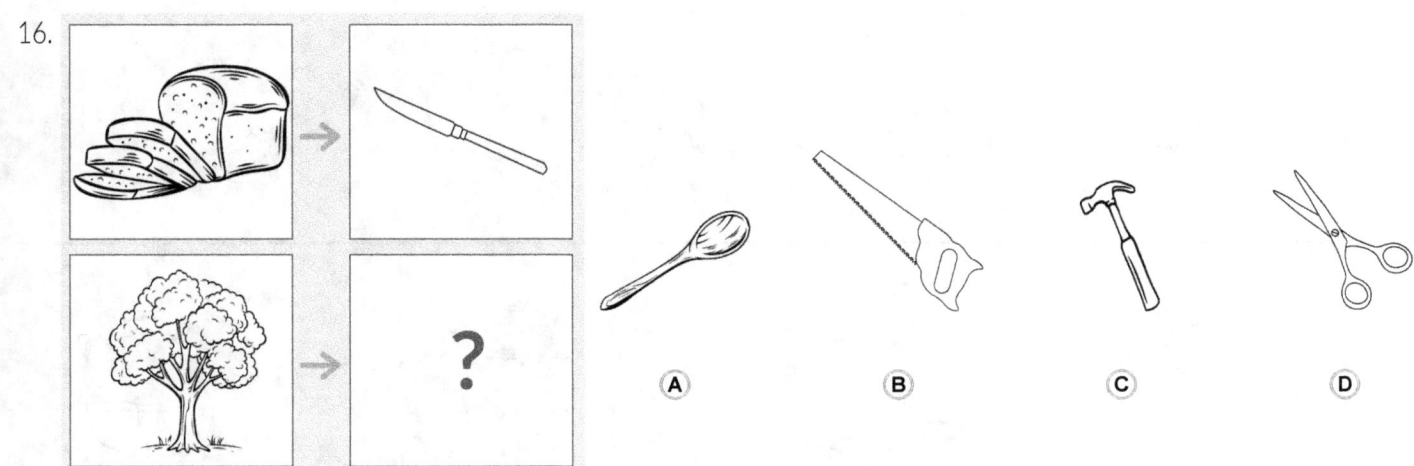

PICTURE CLASSIFICATION

Which one goes best?

Kai

Directions (read to child):

The top row shows three pictures that are alike in some way. Look at the bottom row. There are four pictures. Which picture in the bottom row goes best with the pictures in the top row?

Explanation (for parents):

A more detailed explanation and another Picture Classification example question is on p.8. If you have not already, look over p.8. Following is an excerpt. Together with your child, try to figure out a "rule" describing how the top pictures are alike and belong together. Then, apply the "rule" to each answer choice to determine which one follows it. If your child finds that more than one choice follows the rule, then a more specific rule is needed.

Example (read to child):

Let's look at the pictures on the top row. We see a piano, a violin, and a trumpet. Let's come up with a "rule" to describe how these are each alike or how they belong together.

These are all instruments. Now, let's look at the bottom row. Let's find the answer choice on the bottom that follows this same rule of things that are instruments. We see an open box, a computer, a doll, and a drum.

Which one of these goes best with the top row? Which one of them is an instrument? The drum.

1.

      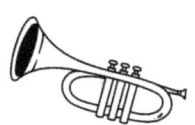

  Ⓐ   Ⓑ   Ⓒ   Ⓓ

2.

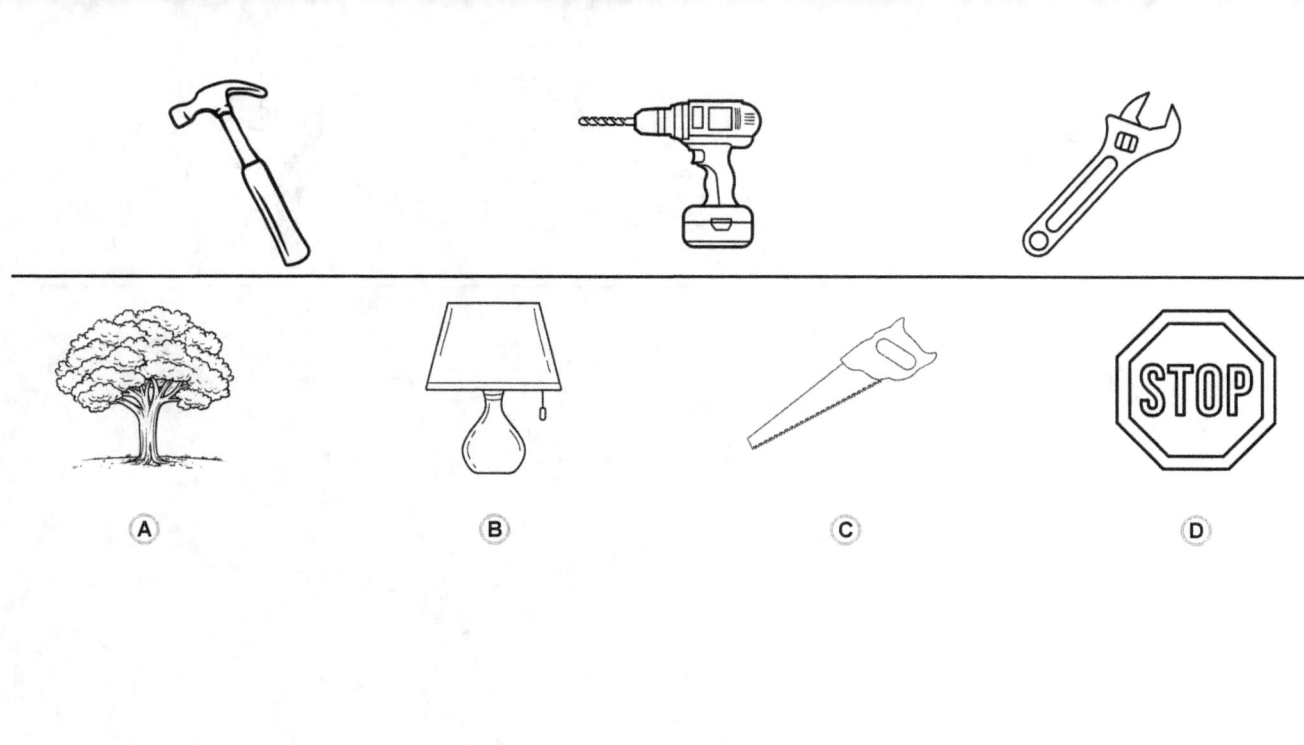

A   B   C   D

3.

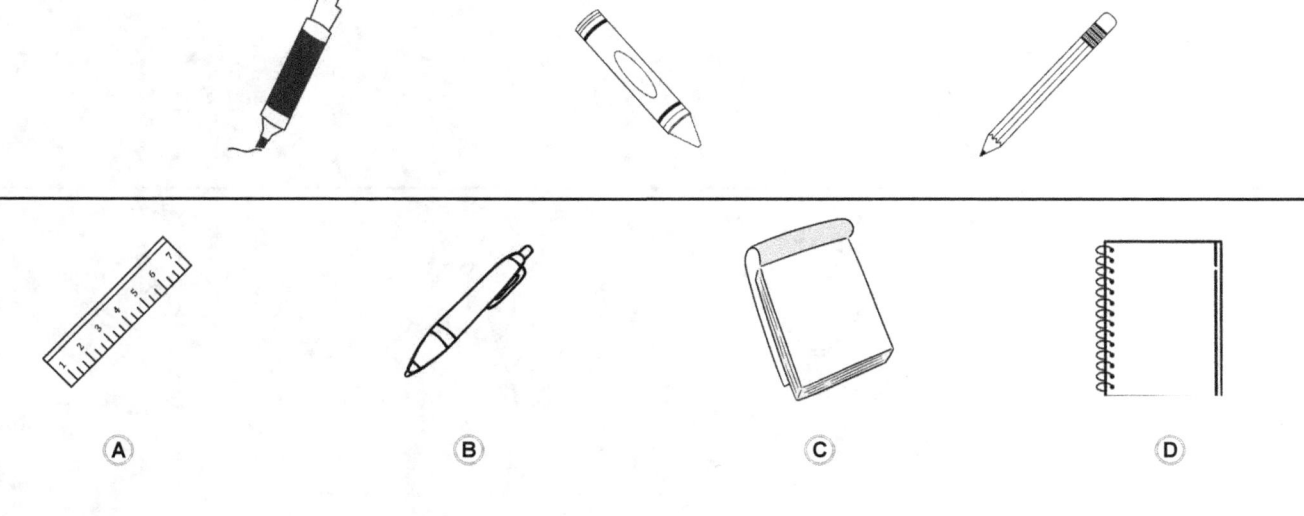

A   B   C   D

4.

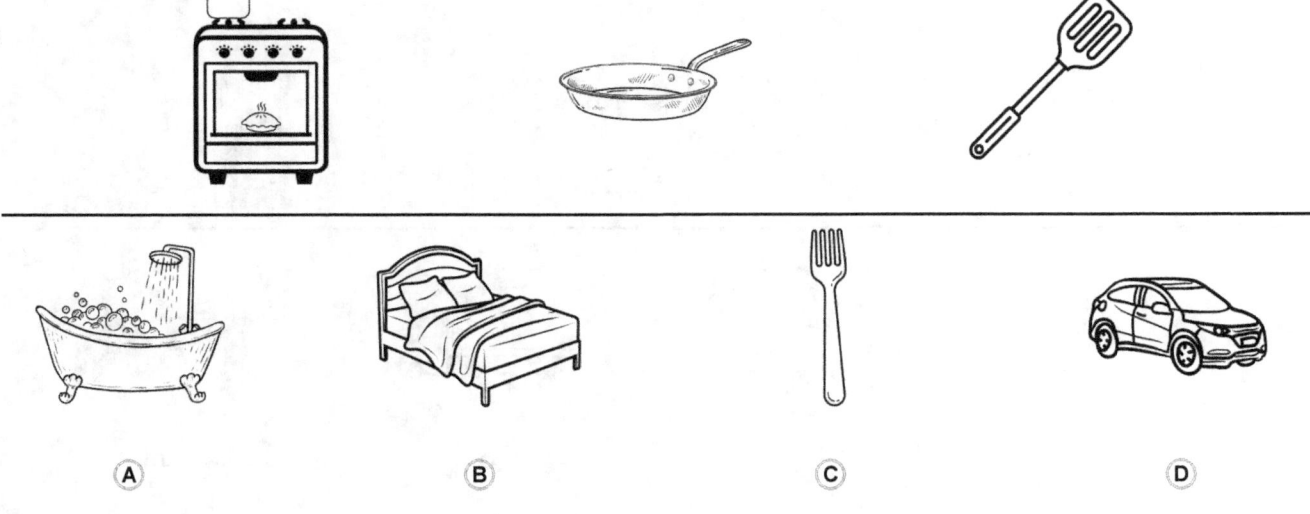

A   B   C   D

5.

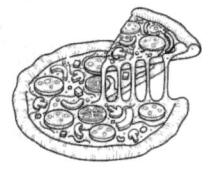 

Ⓐ Ⓑ Ⓒ Ⓓ

6.

Ⓐ Ⓑ Ⓒ Ⓓ

7.

  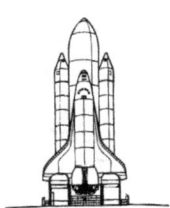

Ⓐ Ⓑ Ⓒ Ⓓ

20

8.

  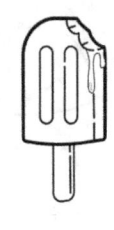 

   A   B   C   D

9.

   A   B   C   D

10.

 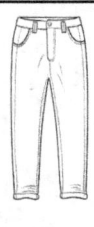  

   A   B   C   D

11.

 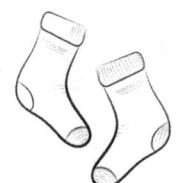 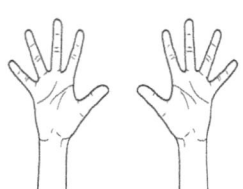

(A)

(B)

(C)

(D)

12.

 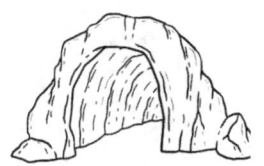 

(A)

(B)

(C)

(D)

13.

  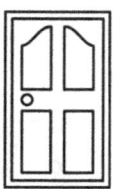

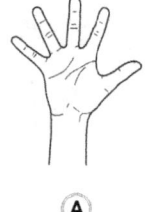

(A)

(B)

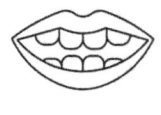

(C)

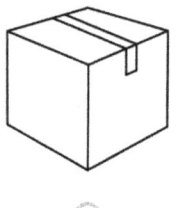

(D)

14.

 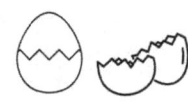 

Ⓐ Ⓑ Ⓒ Ⓓ

15.

Ⓐ Ⓑ Ⓒ Ⓓ

23

16.

  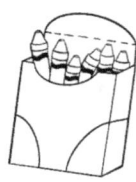 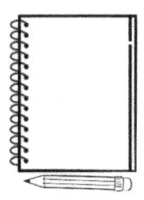

Ⓐ   Ⓑ   Ⓒ   Ⓓ

17.

Ⓐ   Ⓑ   Ⓒ   Ⓓ

Keep up the good work!

Noah

SENTENCE COMPLETION

Listen closely!

Maya

Directions (read to child): Listen to the question, then choose the best answer. I can only read the question one time.

Additional information (for parents): Read the questions in this section to your child.

As explained earlier in the Introduction on p. 10, test administrators will read these questions only one time.

Therefore, it is imperative that your child practice careful listening skills, so that you will not need to repeat the questions.

1. If there was a fire, which vehicle would arrive to help?

A   B   C   D

2. If you were at a grocery store, which of these would you probably not see?

   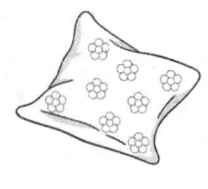      

A   B   C   D

3. If you were skiing down a snowy mountain, which one of these would you be wearing?

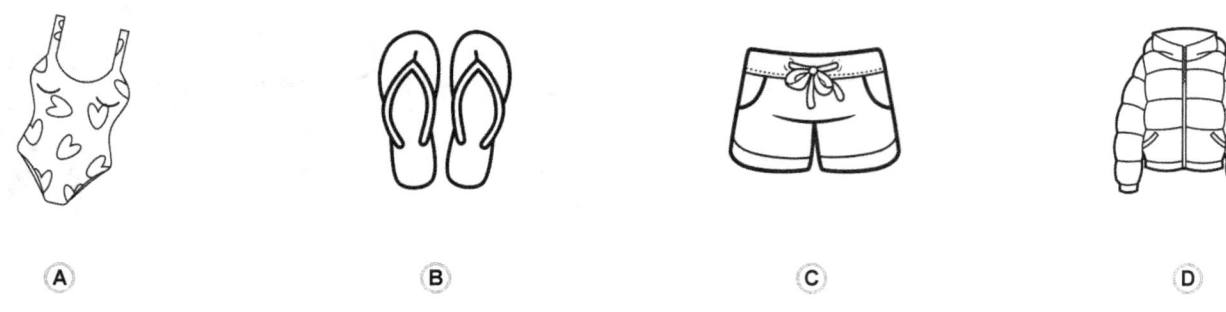

    Ⓐ   Ⓑ   Ⓒ   Ⓓ

4. One of your parents is cutting a branch off a tree. Which tool would they be using?

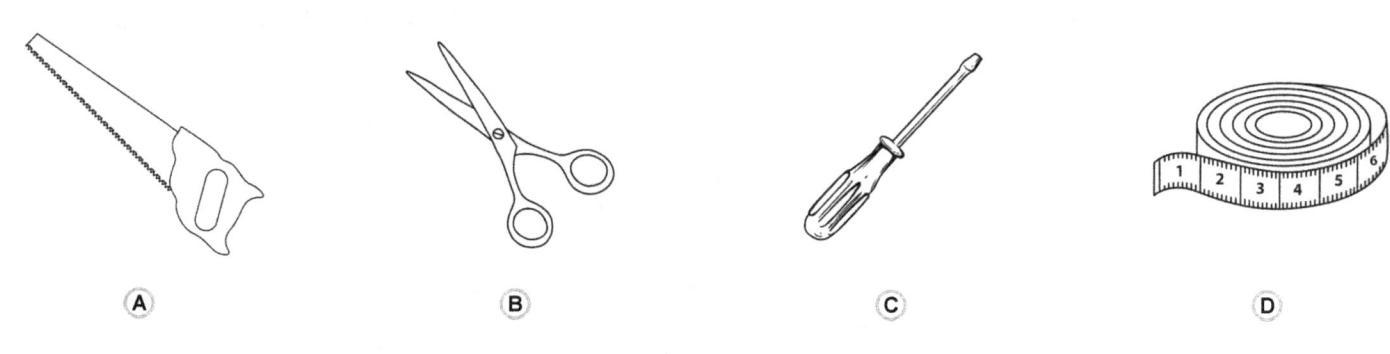

    Ⓐ   Ⓑ   Ⓒ   Ⓓ

5. Your friend is eating a snack that is not very healthy. Which one of these is your friend eating?

    Ⓐ   Ⓑ   Ⓒ   Ⓓ

6. Which one of these grows roots?

A   B   C   D

7. Which of these should you not put in your mouth?

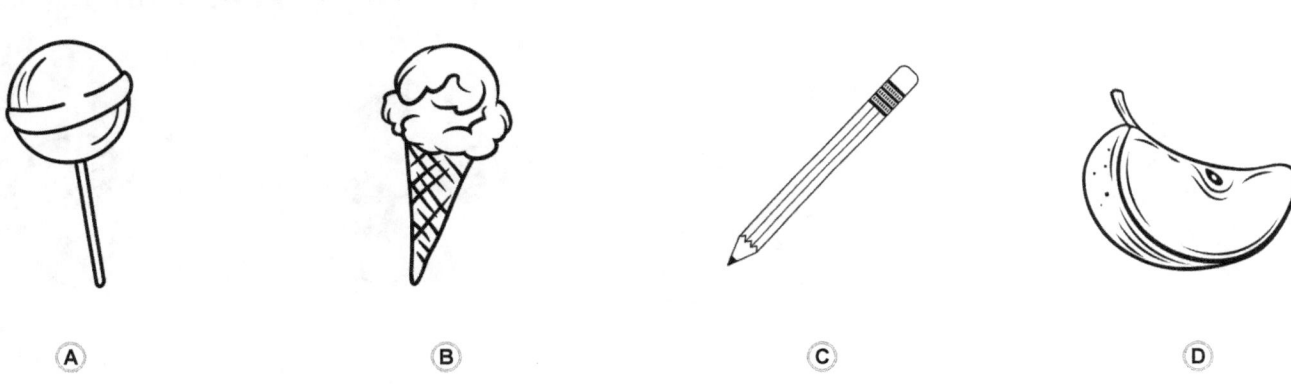

A   B   C   D

8. You are roasting marshmallows with your family. Which one of these would you use?

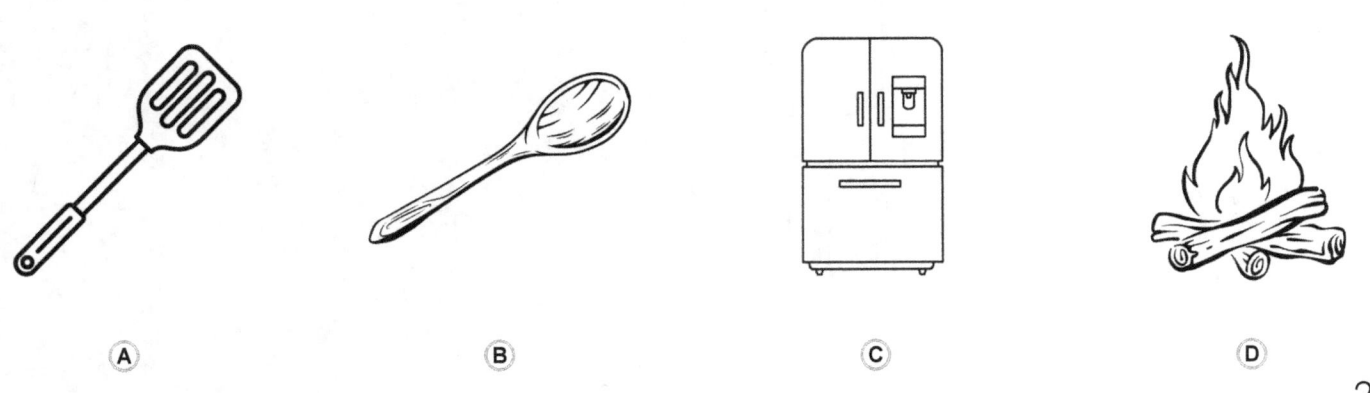

A   B   C   D

9. Your grandpa needs to sew a button on his shirt. Which one would he use?

10. Your friend just kicked a ball and scored a goal. Which one of these did they kick?

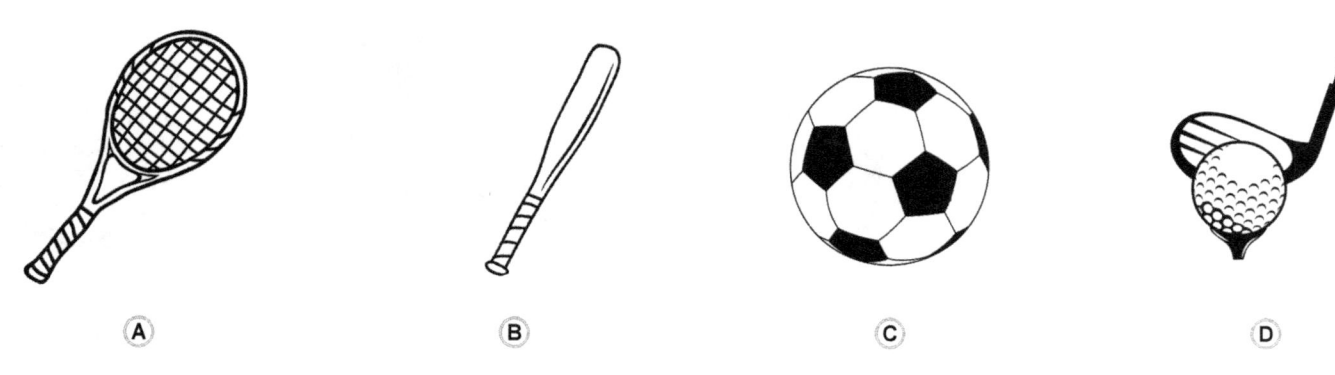

11. Which choice shows 1 living thing and 1 non-living thing?

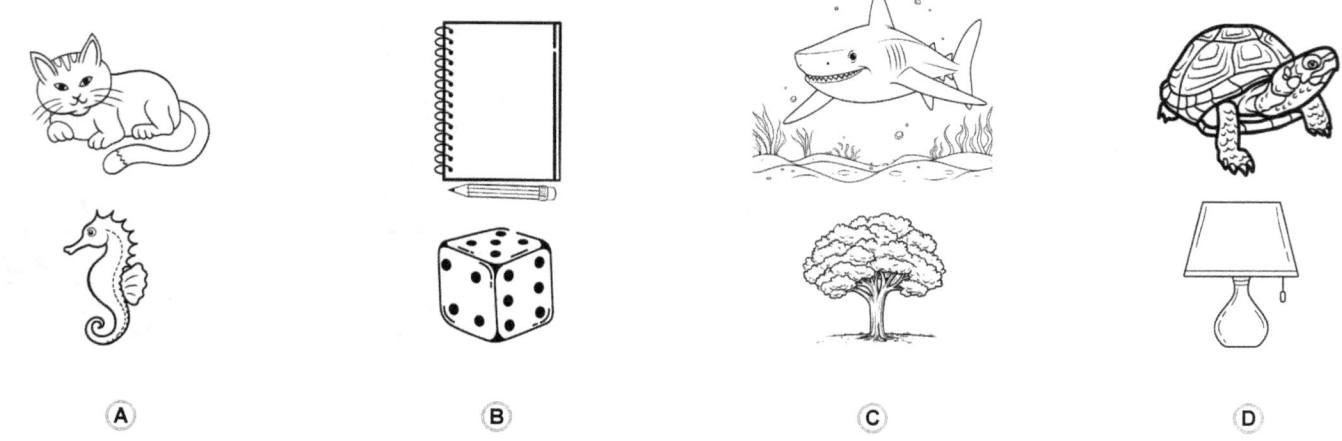

12. You are looking at the plants in a garden. Which of these would you probably not see?

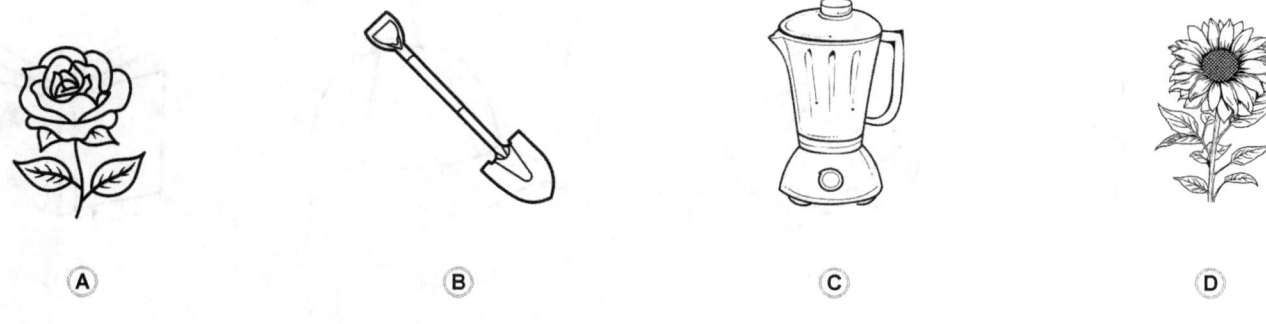

A   B   C   D

13. Which of these would you not see at a bakery?

A   B   C   D

14. You are writing a story about an animal that's extinct. Which one of these could your story be about?

A   B   C   D

15. Which one of these would you have assembled before using?

A   B   C   D

16. Which of these would you use to get rid of a mosquito?

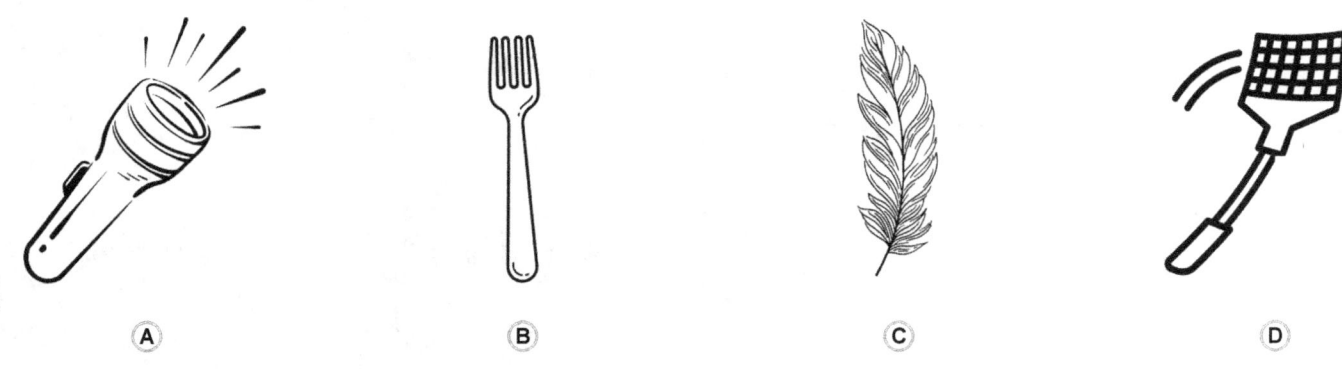

A   B   C   D

- End of Practice Test 1 (Workbook Format) -
- Practice Test 2 begins on the next page. -

Excellent job! You're done with the first part!

Zoe

COGAT® PRACTICE TEST 2

START OF PRACTICE TEST 2 / PICTURE ANALOGIES

Directions: The pictures in the top boxes go together in some way. One of the bottom boxes is empty. Which answer choice goes with the picture in the bottom box in the same way the top pictures do?

1.

A B C D

2.

A B C D

3.

A B C D

4.

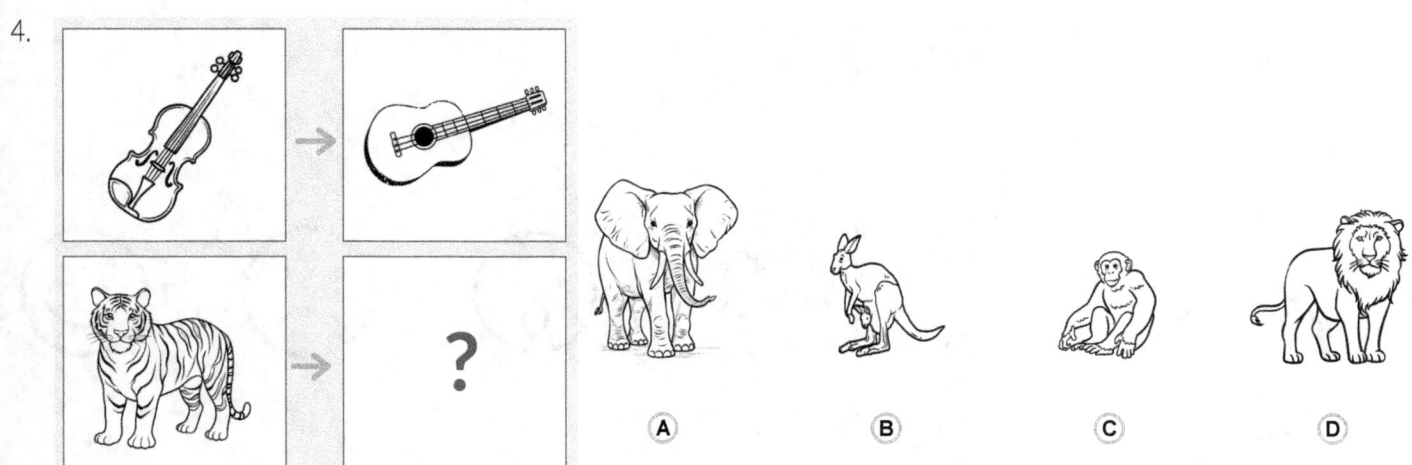

A B C D

5.

A B C D

6.

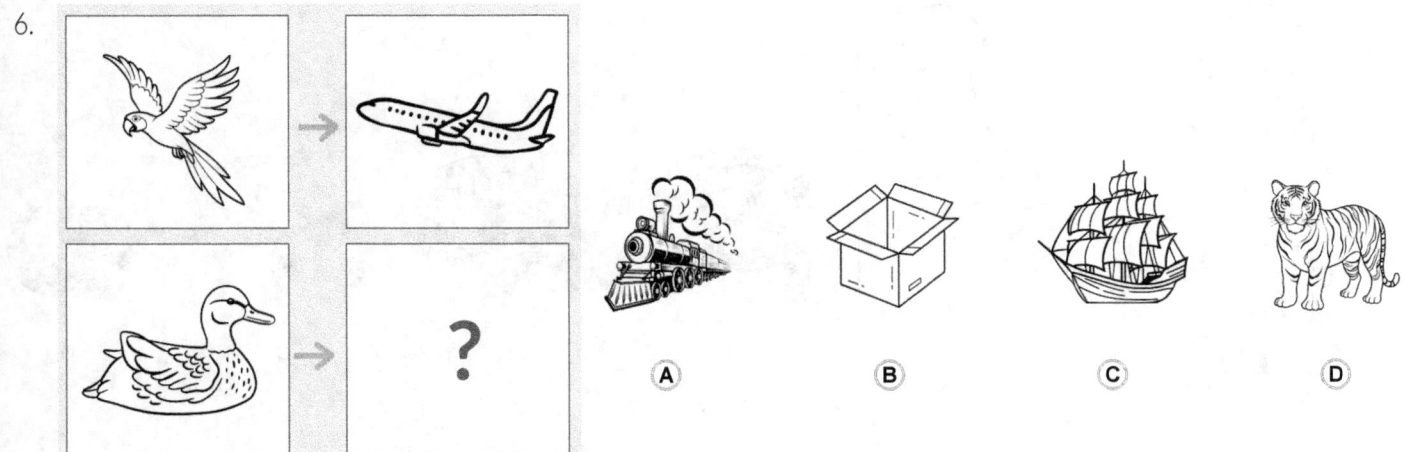

A B C D

7.

(A) (B) (C) (D)

8.

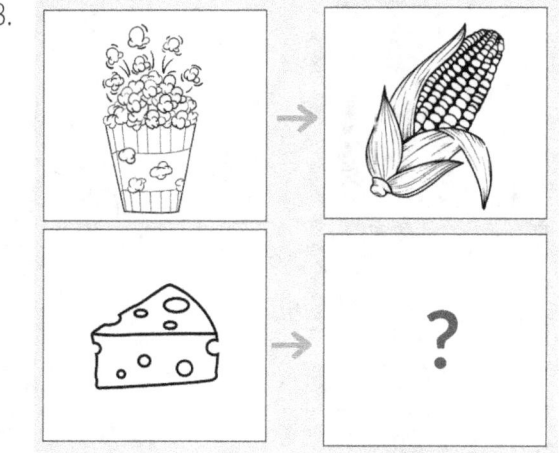

(A) (B) (C) (D)

9.

(A) (B) (C) (D)

10.

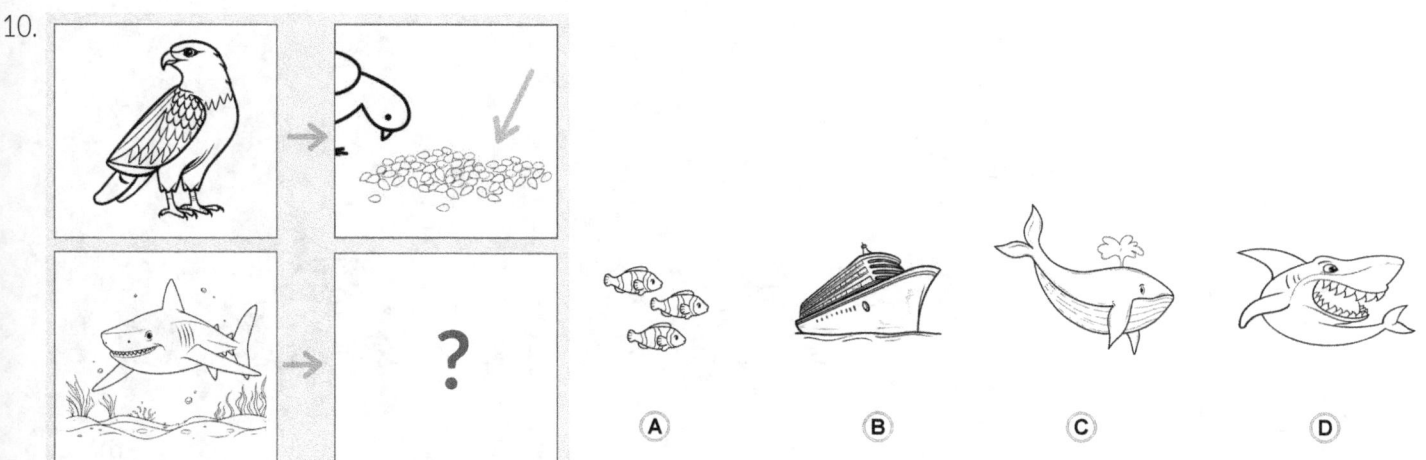

11.

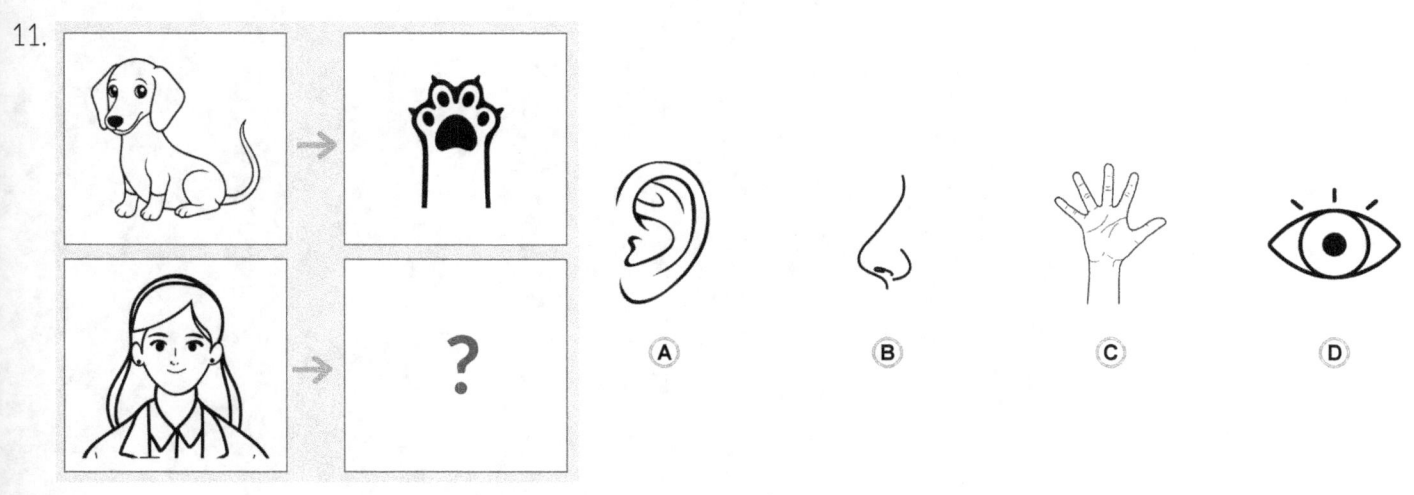

12.

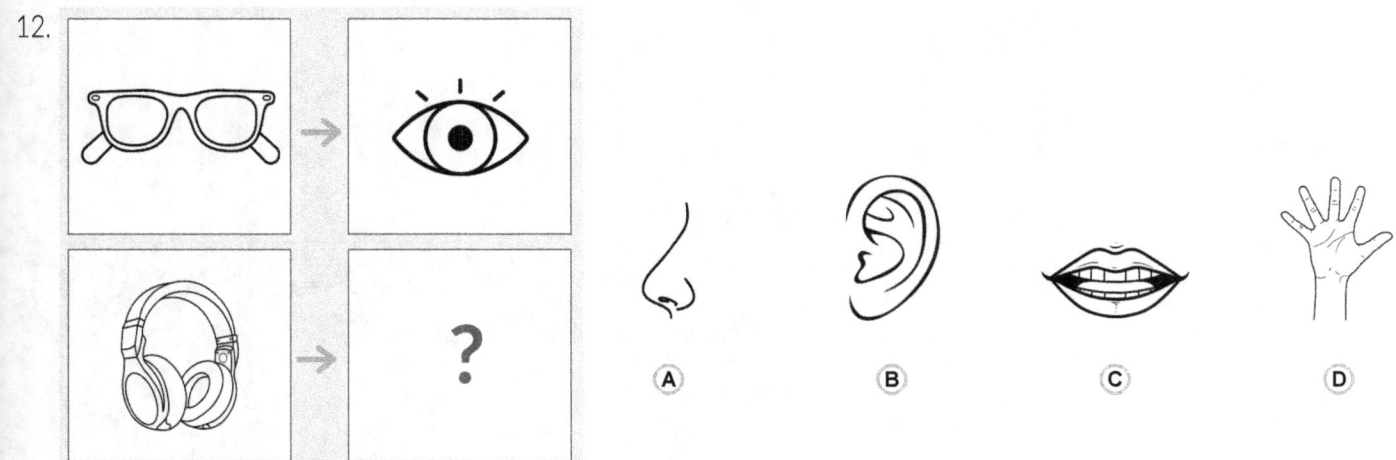

13.

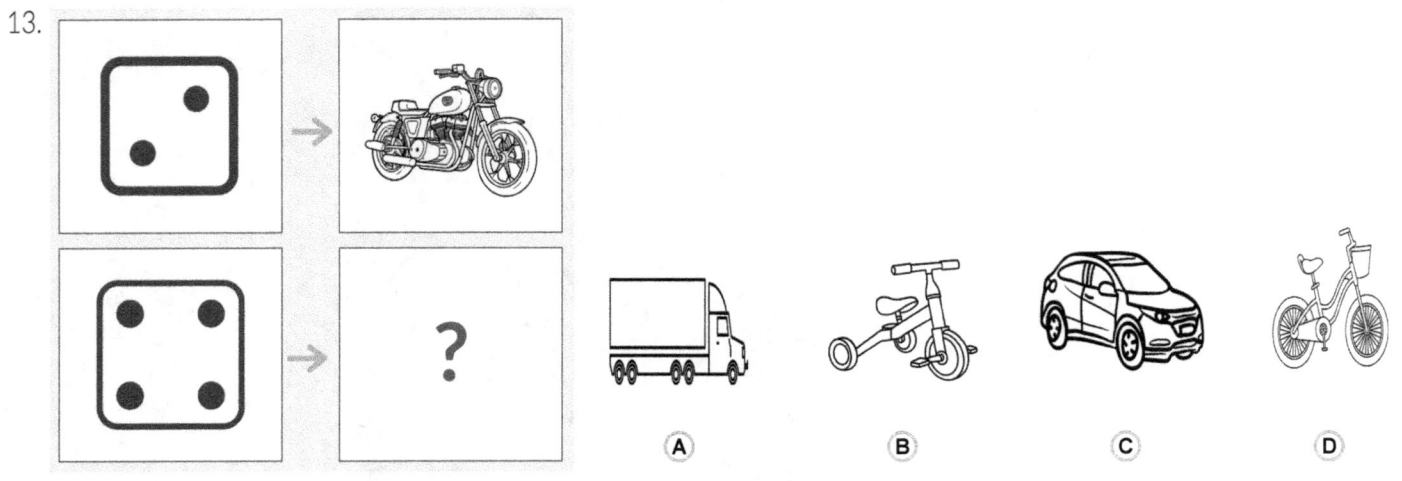

14.

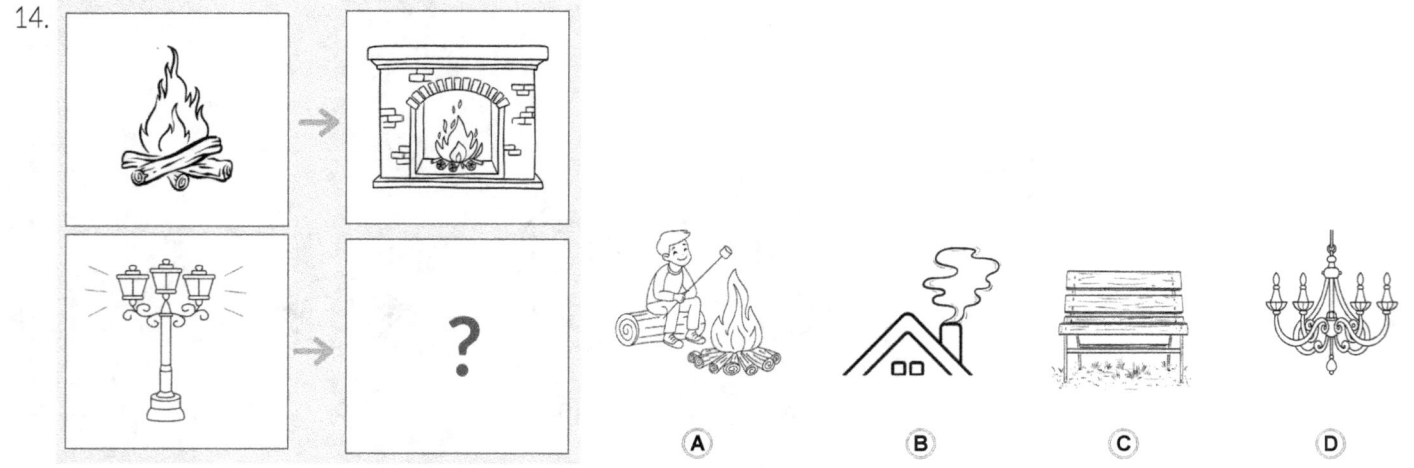

15.

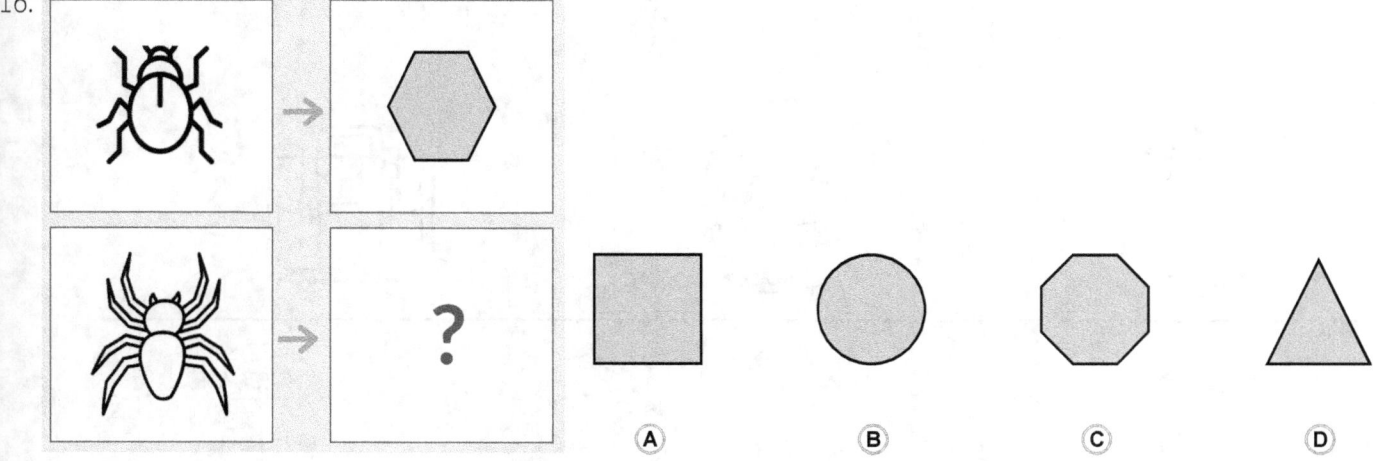

16.

PICTURE CLASSIFICATION
Directions: The top row shows three pictures that are alike in some way. Look at the bottom row. Which bottom picture goes best with the top pictures?

1.

2.

3.

4.

(A) (B) (C) (D)

5.

(A) (B) (C) (D)

6.

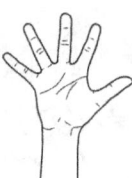  

(A) (B) (C) (D)

7.

(A) (B) (C) (D)

8.

  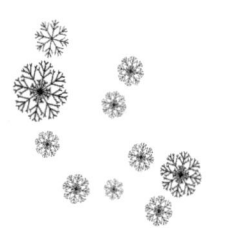

(A) (B) (C) (D)

9.

(A) (B) (C) (D)

10.

Ⓐ　　　　　Ⓑ　　　　　Ⓒ　　　　　Ⓓ

11.

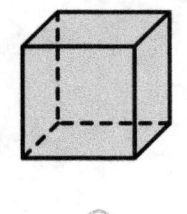 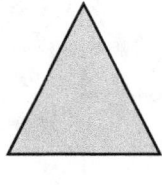 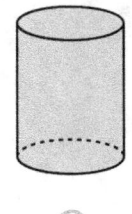 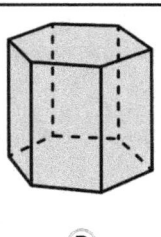

Ⓐ　　　　　Ⓑ　　　　　Ⓒ　　　　　Ⓓ

12.

Ⓐ　　　　　Ⓑ　　　　　Ⓒ　　　　　Ⓓ

13.

　　　　　　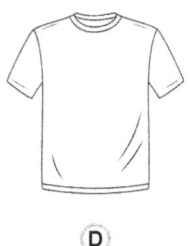

Ⓐ　　　　　Ⓑ　　　　　Ⓒ　　　　　Ⓓ

14.

Ⓐ　　　　　Ⓑ　　　　　Ⓒ　　　　　Ⓓ

15.

 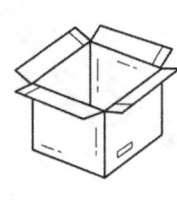  

(A) (B) (C) (D)

16.

(A) (B) (C) (D)

SENTENCE COMPLETION

Directions: Listen to the question, then choose the best answer.

1. If you were baking cookies, which of these would you need?

(A)

(B)

(C)

(D)

2. If you needed to check the temperature outside, which one would you use?

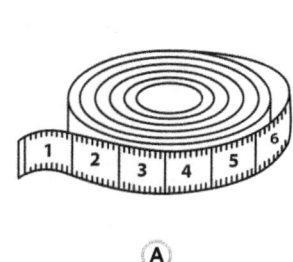
(A)

(B)

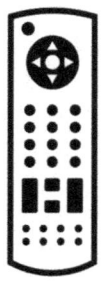
(C)

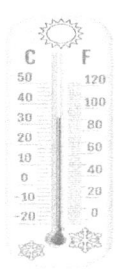
(D)

3. If you were getting dressed on a cold winter day, which item would you wear?

(A)

(B)

(C)

(D)

4. If you needed to find a scent, what body part would you use?

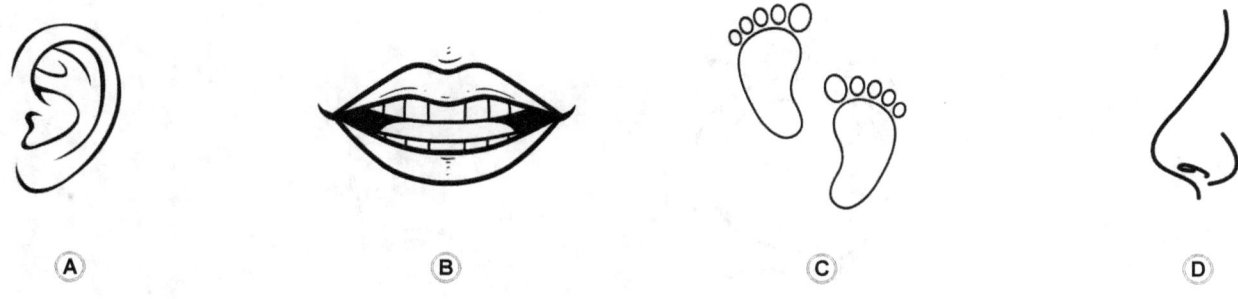

A   B   C   D

5. If you wanted to see a bird that was flying far away, which of these would be the best choice?

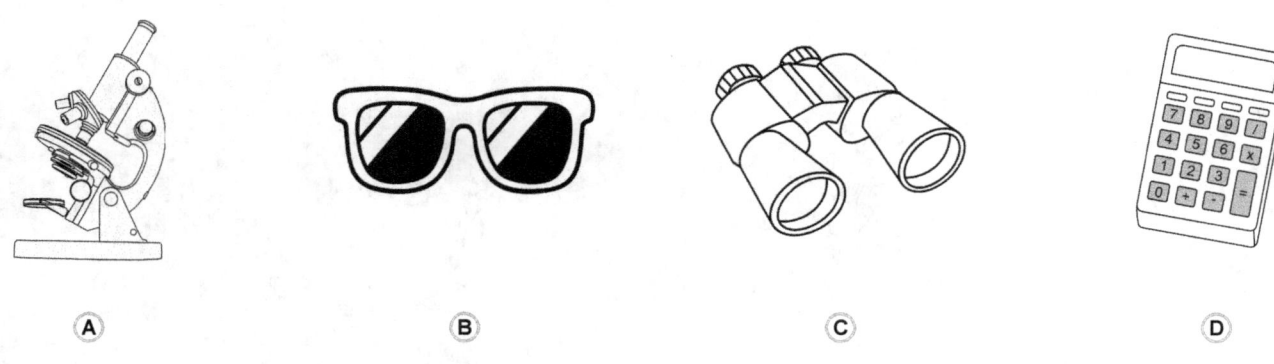

A   B   C   D

6. Which picture shows an animal that does not live in the ocean?

A   B   C   D

7. If you were looking at a map, which one of these would you use to find direction?

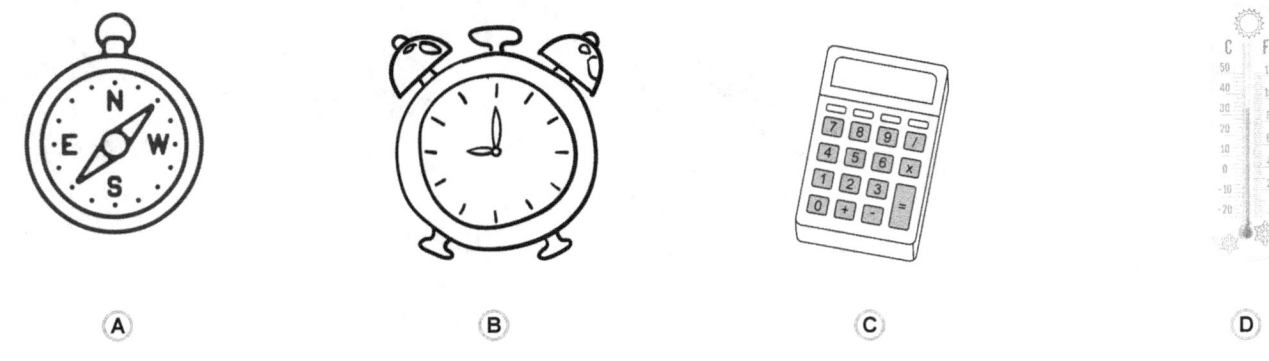

A   B   C   D

8. Which of these animals can fly?

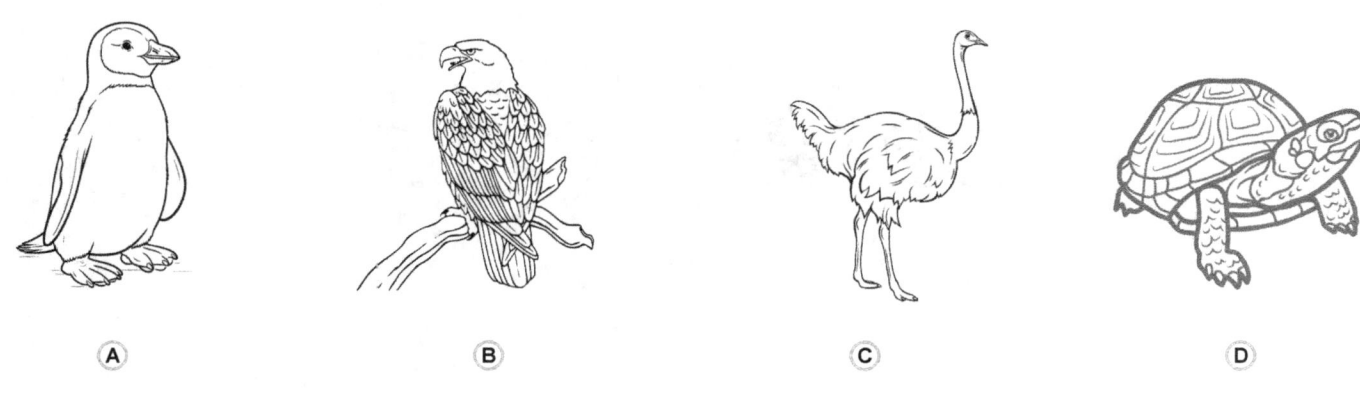

A   B   C   D

9. If you want to see in the dark, which of these would be the most helpful?

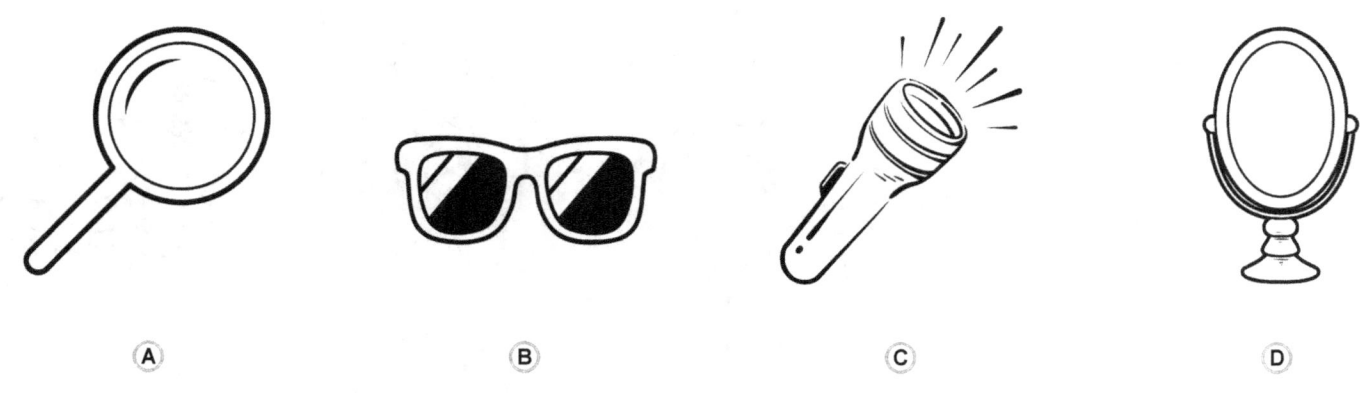

A   B   C   D

10. If someone needed to cut a piece of paper, which one of these should they use?

11. Which one of these would put out a fire?

12. Your friend has a pet that is a type of reptile. Which of these animals is your friend's pet?

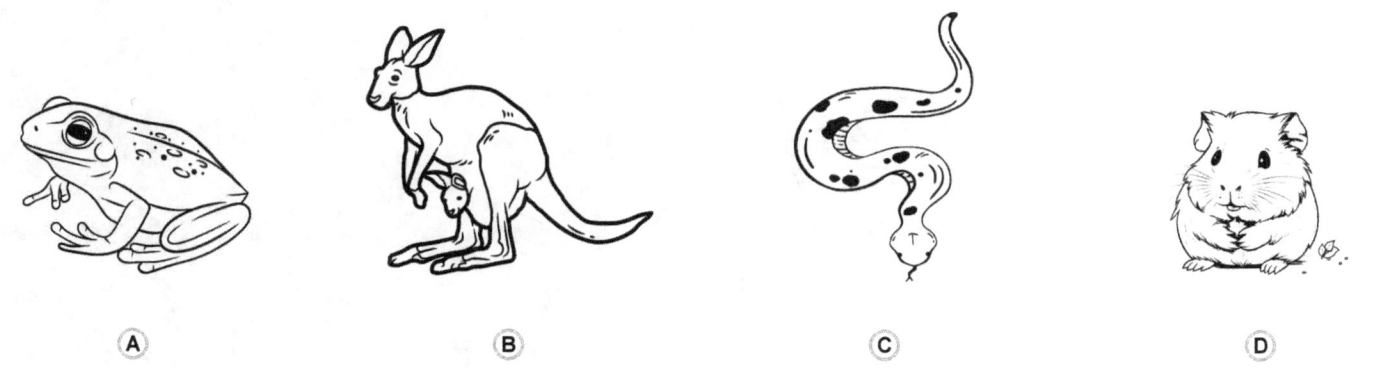

13. You need to check your reflection. Which of these objects would you use to do that?

(A)   (B)   (C)   (D)

14. There are 2 drinks on a table. One is a hot drink and one is a cold drink. Which picture shows the 2 things?

(A)   (B)   (C)   (D)

15. There are 2 types of food on a table. One is a food picked from a tree. One is a food that grows on a vine. Which picture shows the 2 types of food?

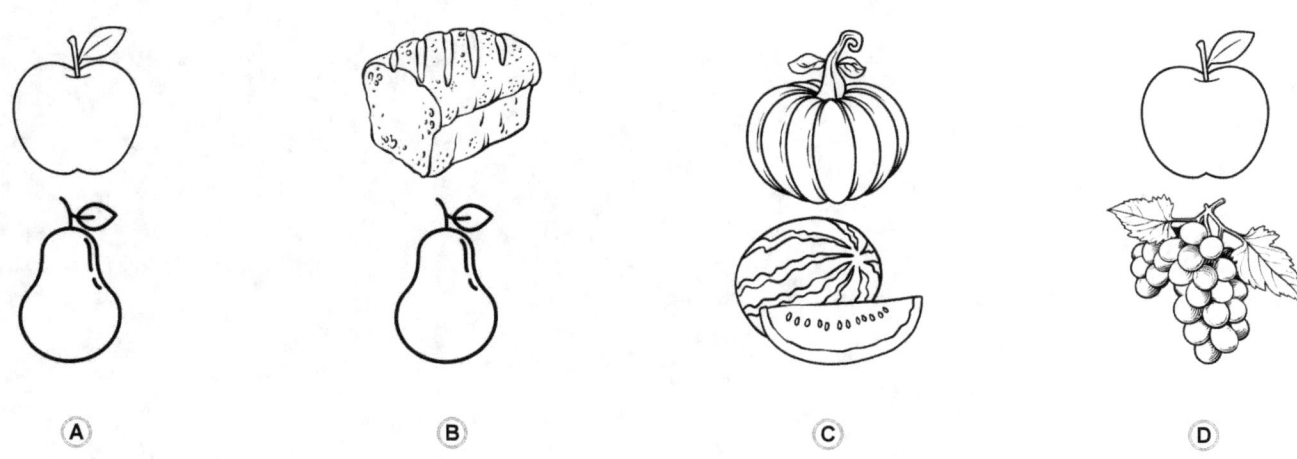

A   B   C   D

16. Which of these could not be used to make something look larger?

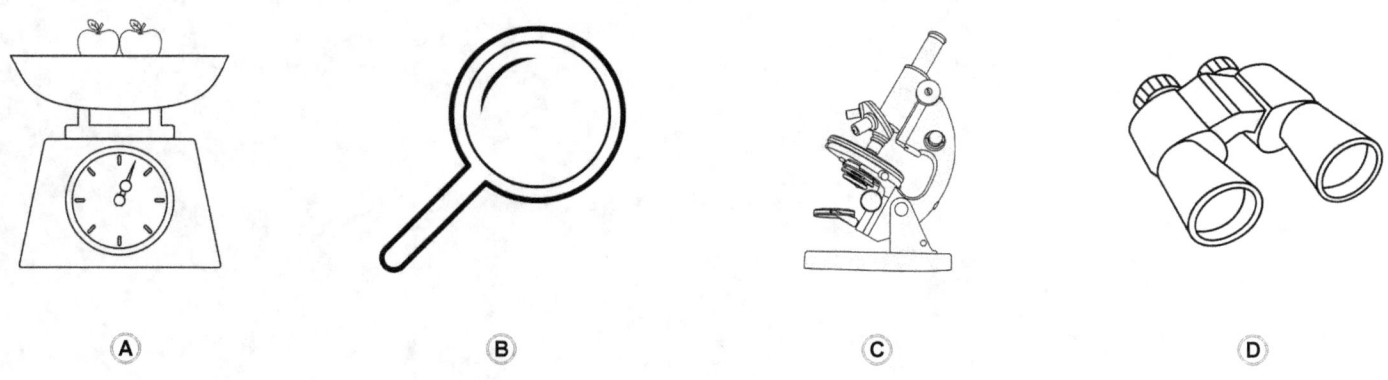

A   B   C   D

- End of Practice Test 2. -

COGAT® PRACTICE TEST 3

START OF PRACTICE TEST 3 / PICTURE ANALOGIES

Directions: The pictures in the top boxes go together in some way. One of the bottom boxes is empty. Which answer choice goes with the picture in the bottom box in the same way the top pictures do?

1.

A   B   C   D

2.

A   B   C   D

3.

A   B   C   D

4.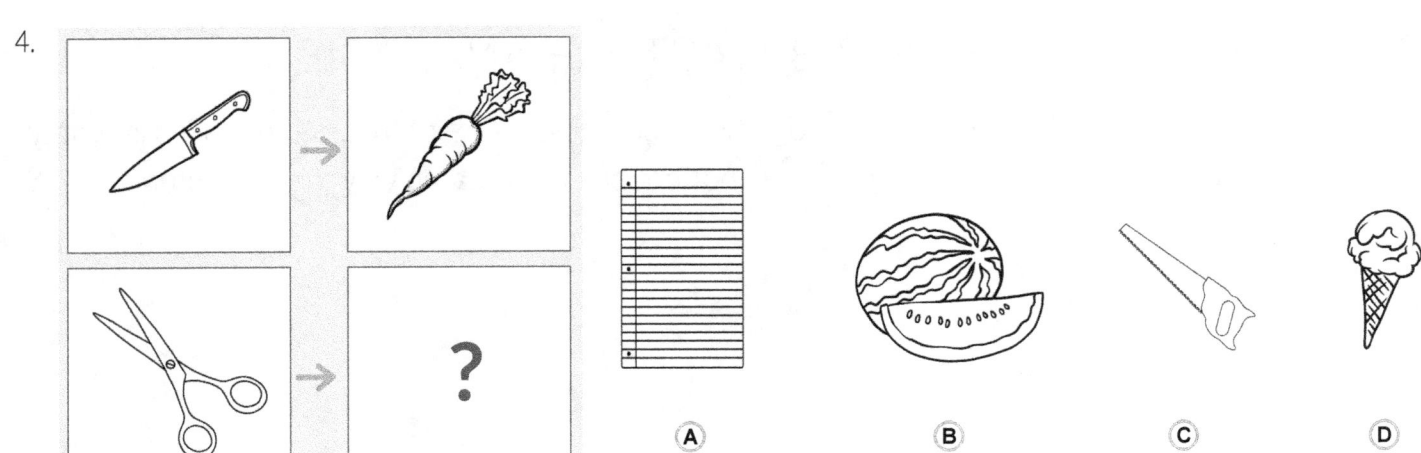

5.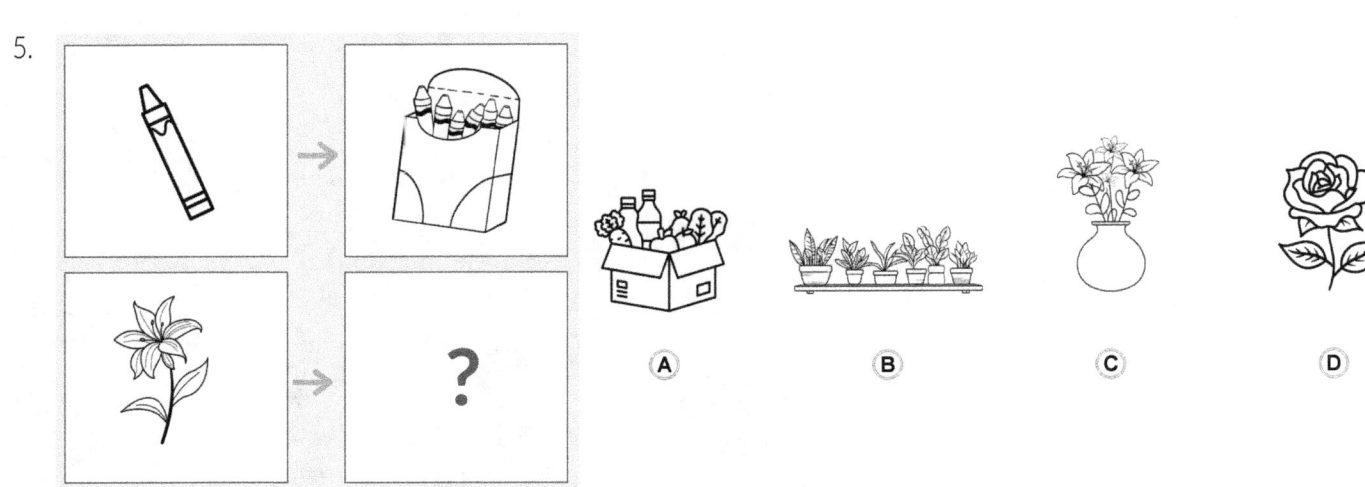

6.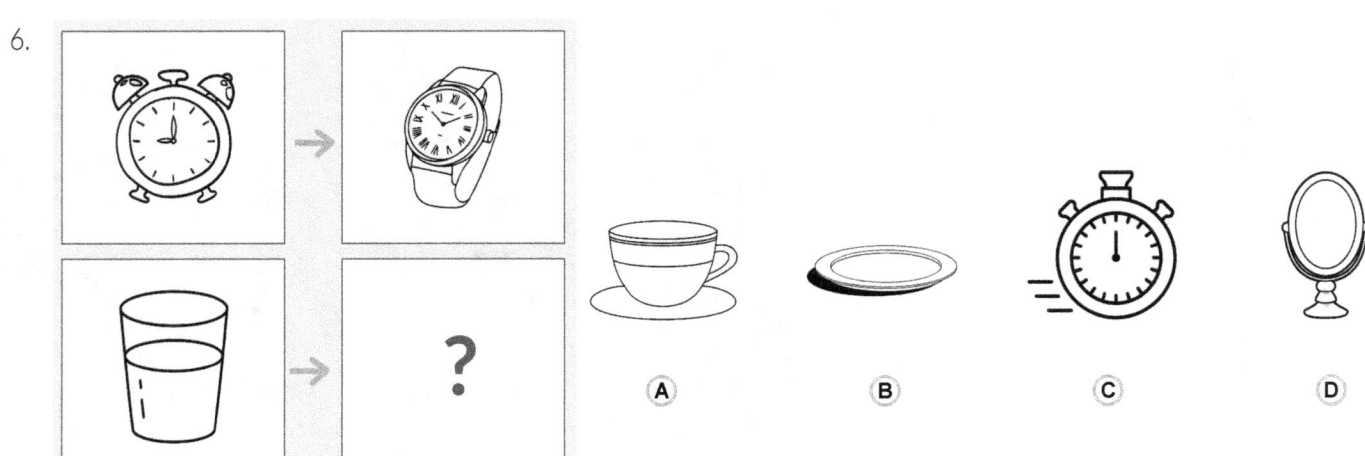

52

7.

8.

9.

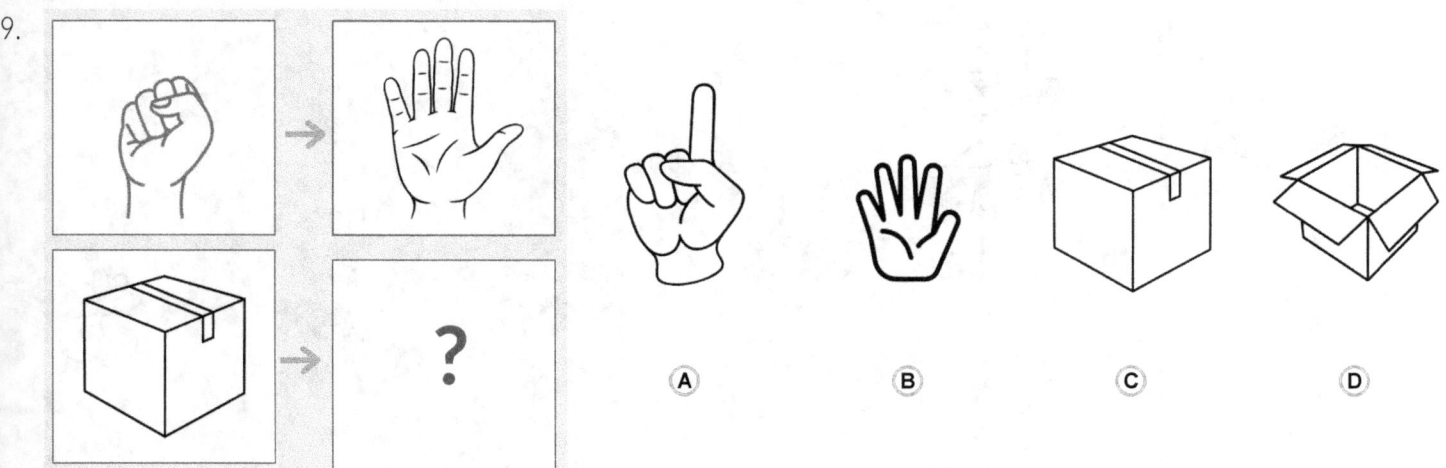

10.

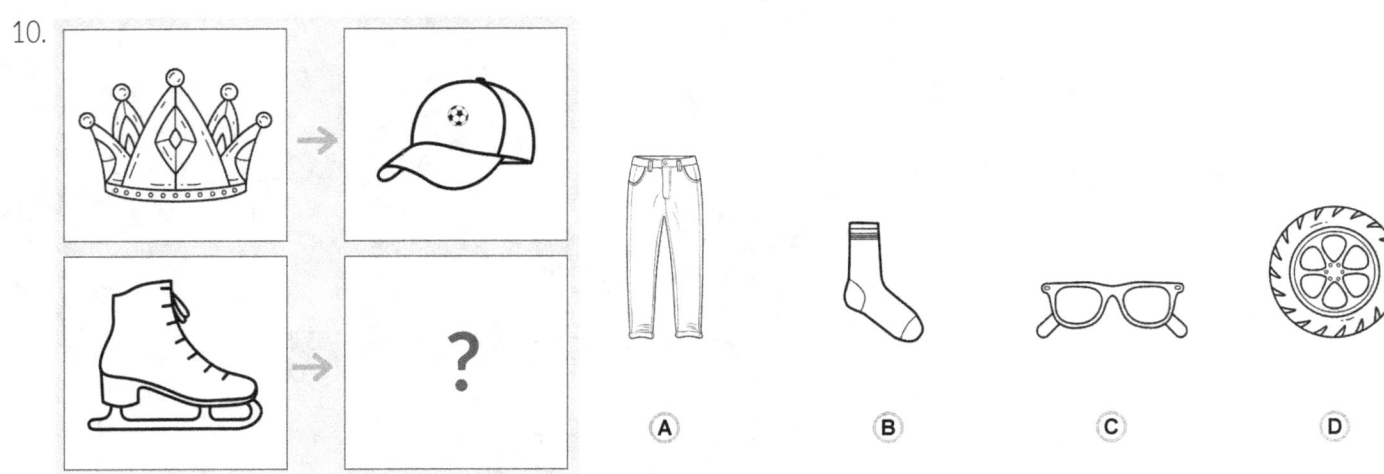

11.

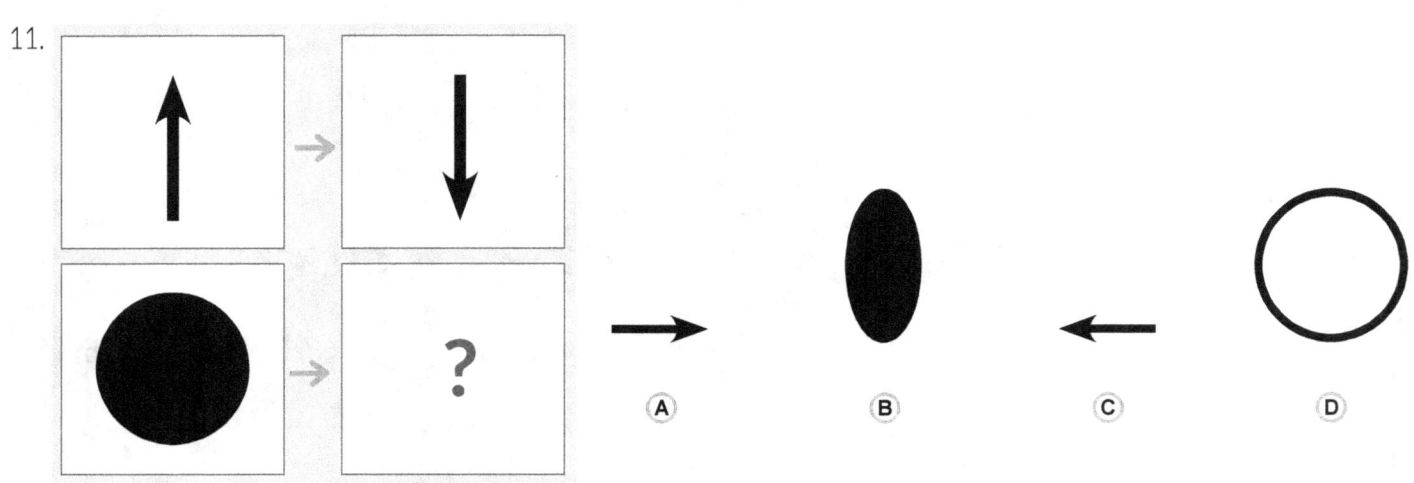

12.

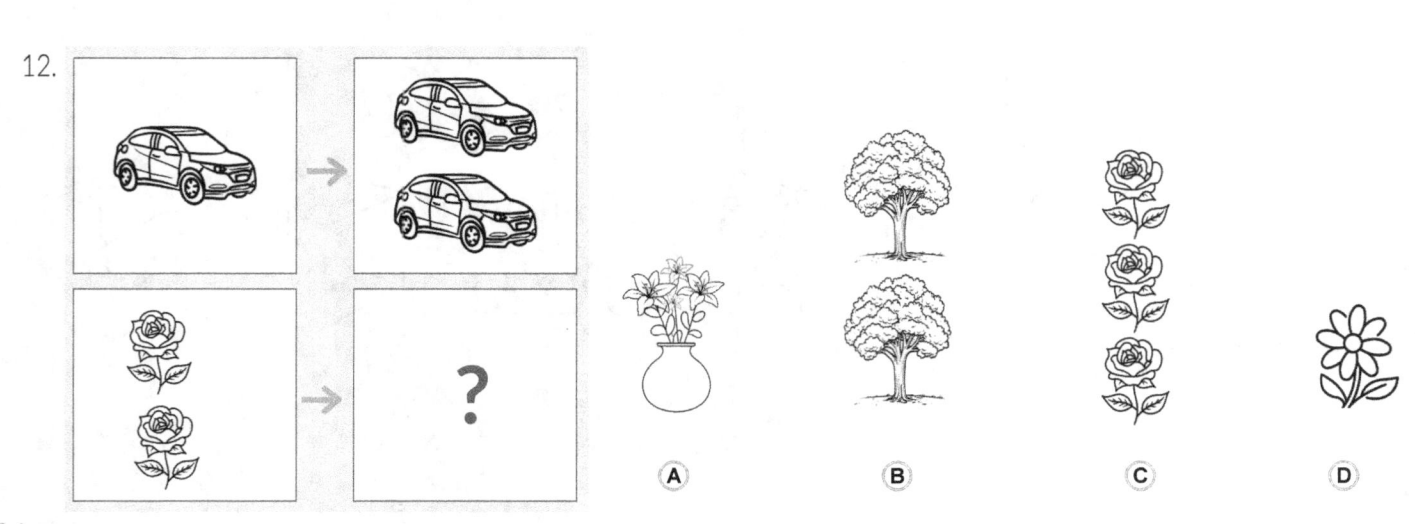

13.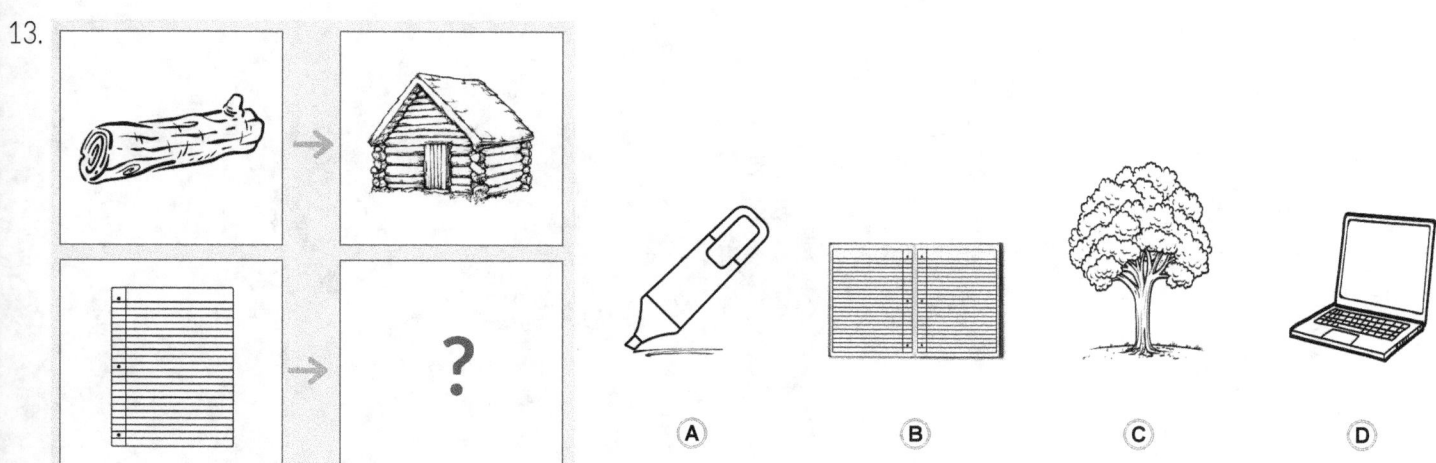

14.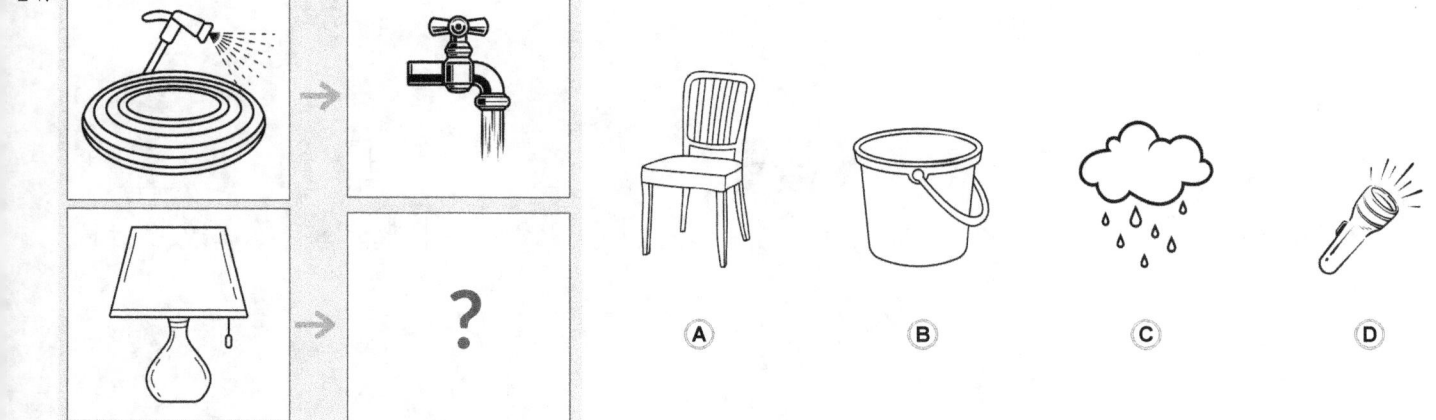

15.

16.

PICTURE CLASSIFICATION

Directions: The top row shows three pictures that are alike in some way. Look at the bottom row. Which bottom picture goes best with the top pictures?

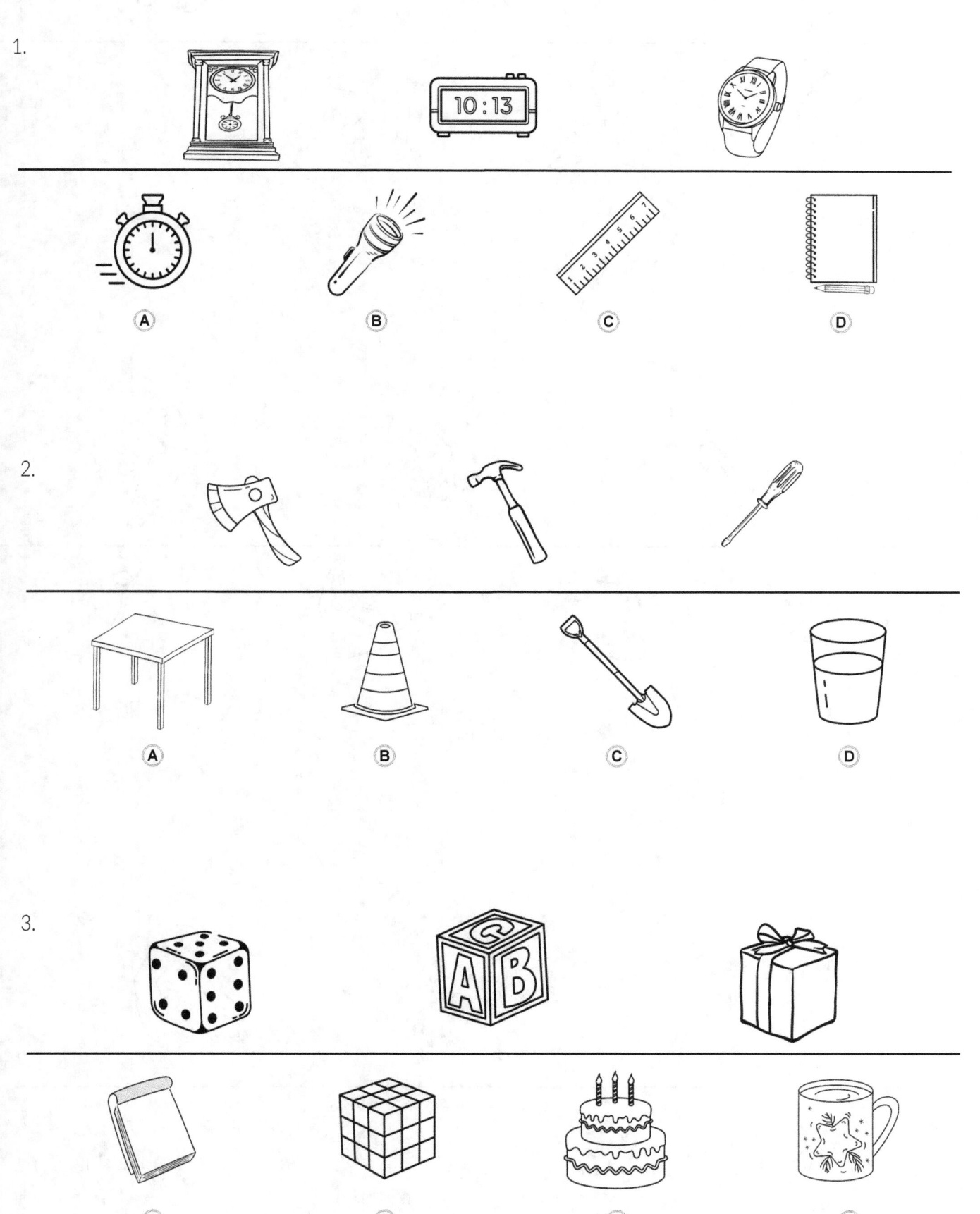

1.

A   B   C   D

2.

A   B   C   D

3.

A   B   C   D

4.

(A) (B) (C) (D)

5.

(A) (B) (C) (D)

6.

(A) (B) (C) (D)

7.

Ⓐ Ⓑ Ⓒ Ⓓ

8.

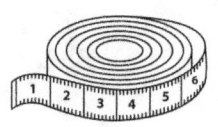 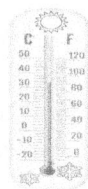 

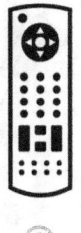 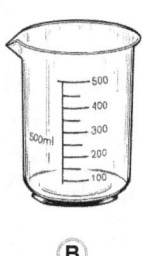 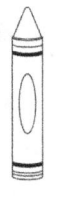 

Ⓐ Ⓑ Ⓒ Ⓓ

9.

  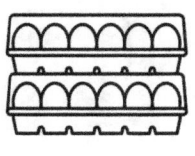 

Ⓐ Ⓑ Ⓒ Ⓓ

10.

 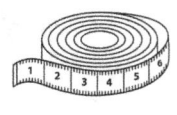 

(A)   (B)   (C)   (D)

11.

(A)   (B)   (C)   (D)

12.

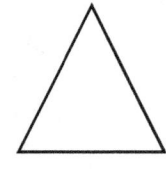  

(A)   (B)   (C)   (D)

13.

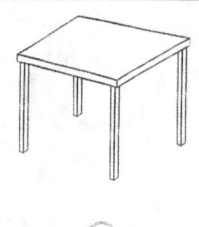  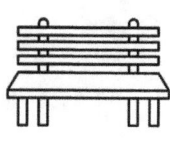 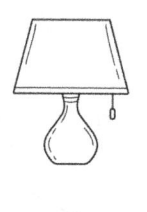

(A) (B) (C) (D)

14.

  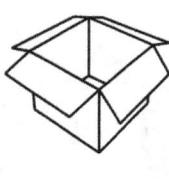 

(A) (B) (C) (D)

15.

 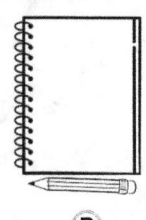  

(A) (B) (C) (D)

SENTENCE COMPLETION

Directions: Listen to the question, then choose the best answer.

1. If you were painting an art project, which item would be the most helpful?

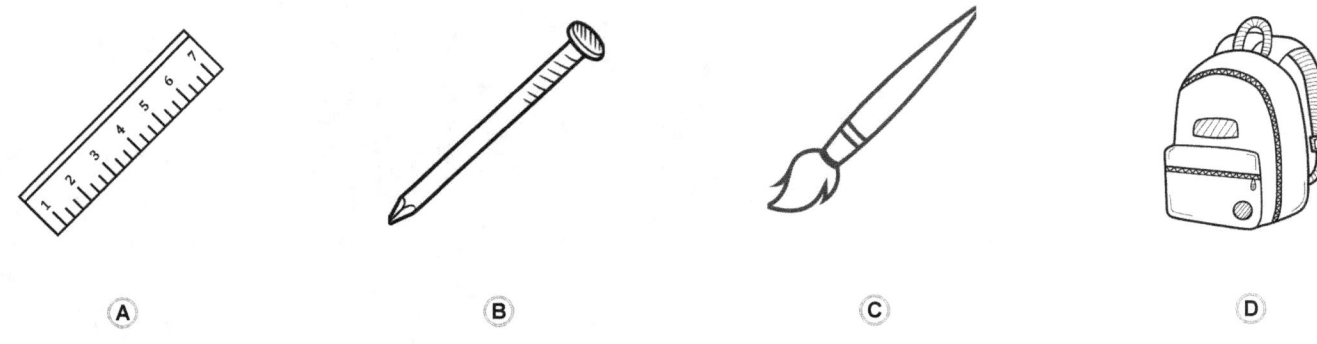

A   B   C   D

2. You are reading a book about an animal that howls. Which animal is your book about?

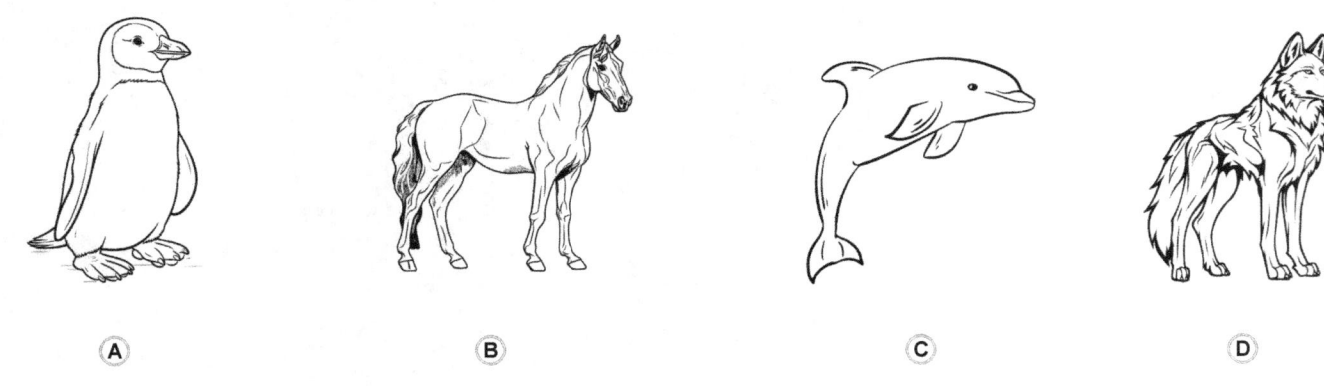

A   B   C   D

3. If you were playing the drums, which item would be the most useful?

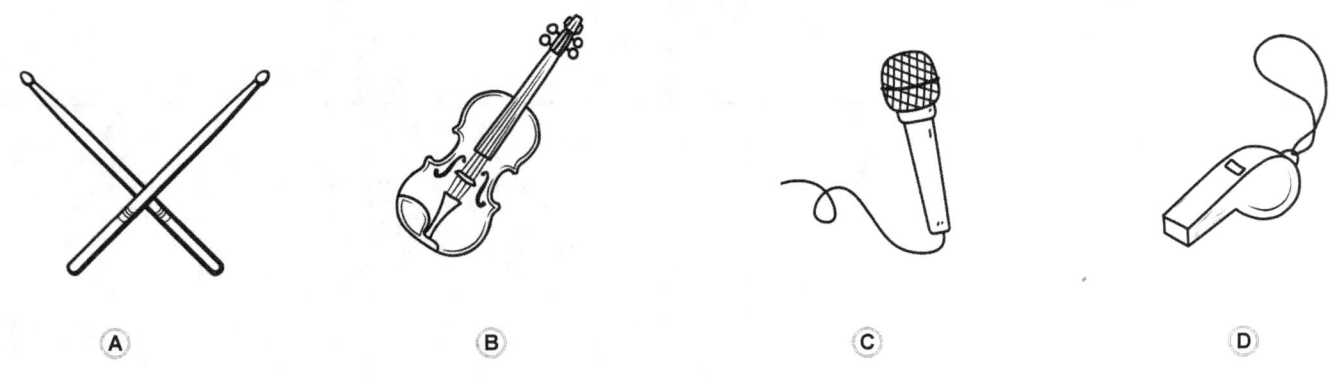

A   B   C   D

4. Which of these objects would you use to water plants?

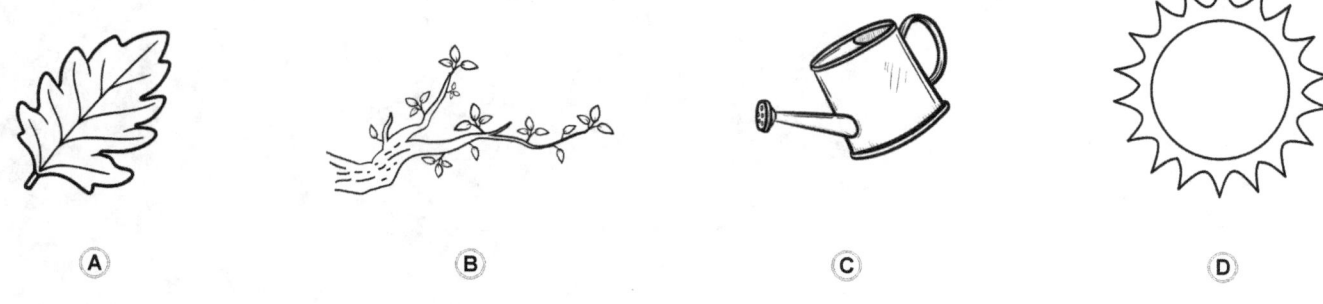

A   B   C   D

5. If you needed to open a locked door, which item would be the most useful?

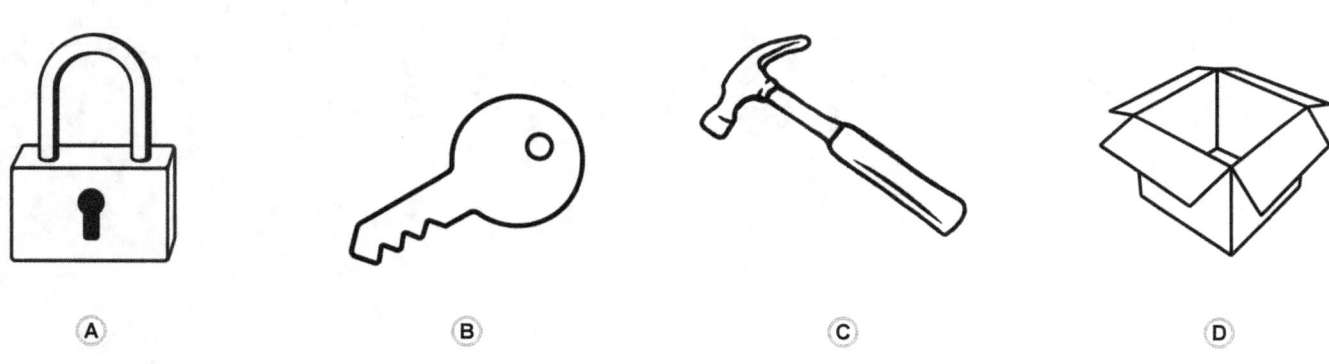

A   B   C   D

6. Your teacher had to sign a piece of paper. Which of these did your teacher use to do this?

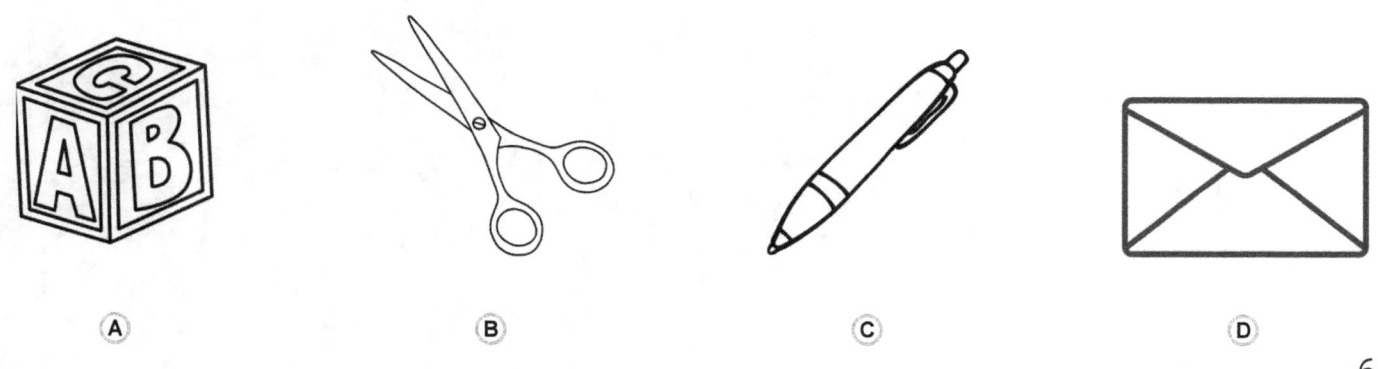

A   B   C   D

7. You have to write a story about an animal that hibernates. Which of these would you choose?

8. Your friend's favorite animal lives on land and cannot fly. Which picture shows your friend's favorite animal?

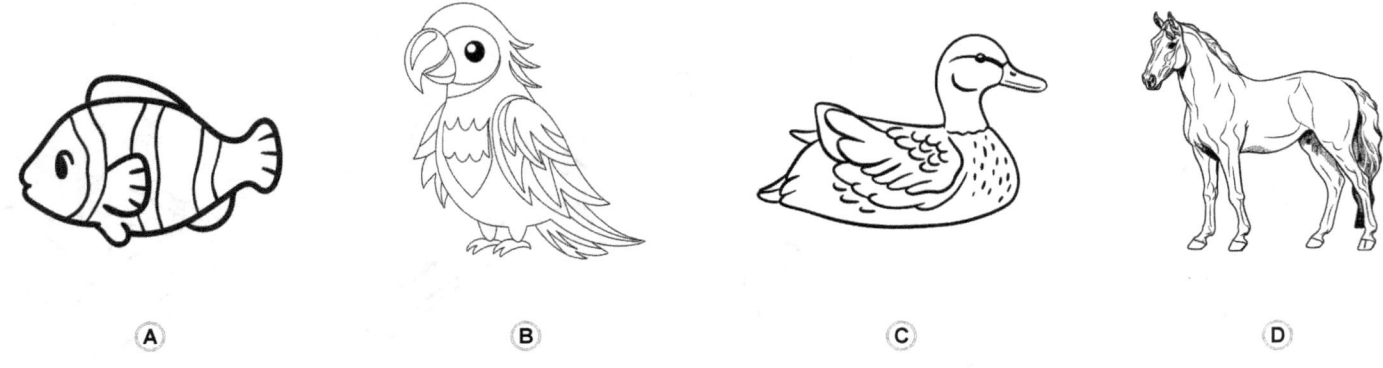

9. Here is a picture of an apple, a pizza, and a cookie. *Point to the next picture >*

Which answer choice below shows this: half of an apple, a whole pizza, and half of a cookie?

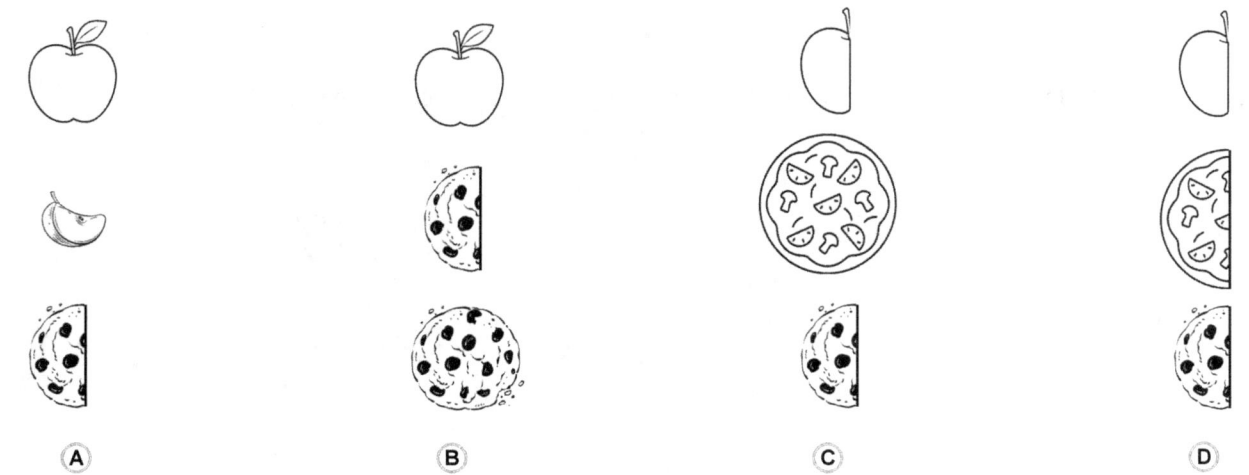

64

10. If you were in the desert, which one of these would you probably see?

    Ⓐ   Ⓑ   Ⓒ   Ⓓ

11. Which picture shows this: Something to read on top, something to write with in the middle, and something to cut with on the bottom?

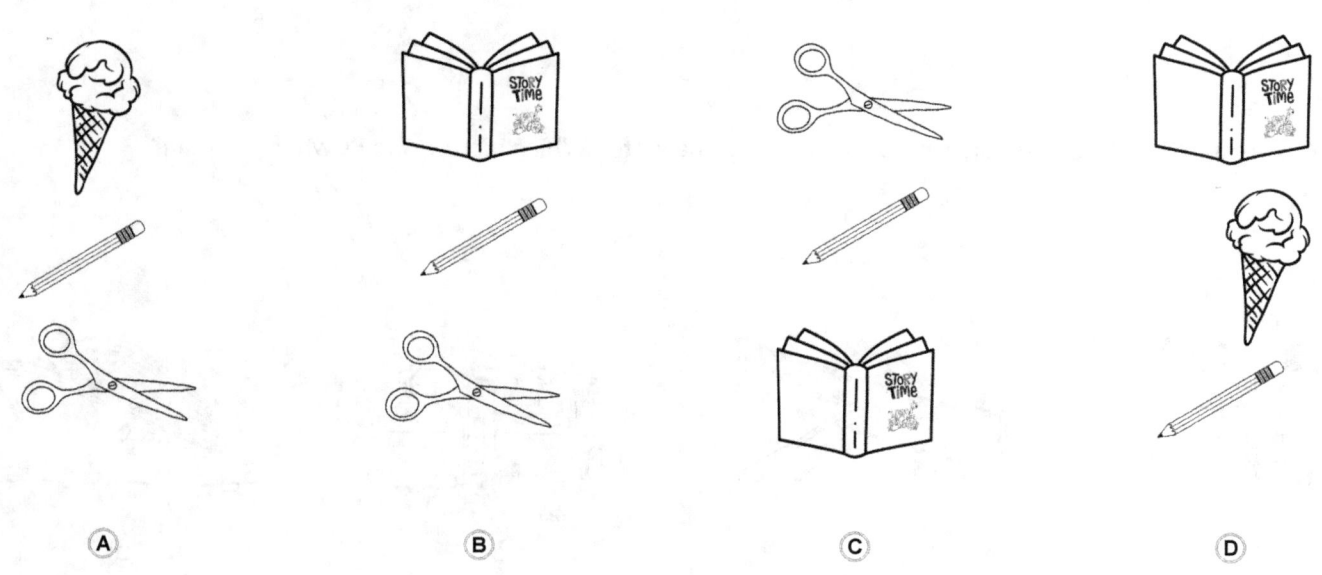

    Ⓐ   Ⓑ   Ⓒ   Ⓓ

12. Dev's favorite animal hatches from an egg. Which picture shows his favorite animal?

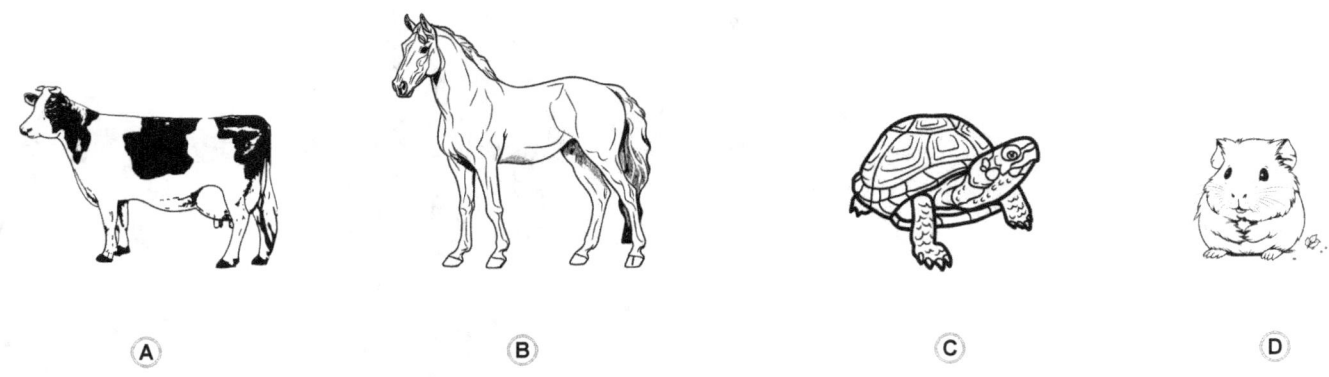

(A)   (B)   (C)   (D)

13. If you were eating a fruit that needed to be peeled first, which one of these were you eating?

(A)   (B)   (C)   (D)

14. You are in something that carries a lot of people in the water. Which picture shows what you're in?

(A)   (B)   (C)   (D)

15. Which picture shows one thing that travels on land and another thing that travels in the air?

| A | B | C | D |

16. Which one of these would a baby not use?

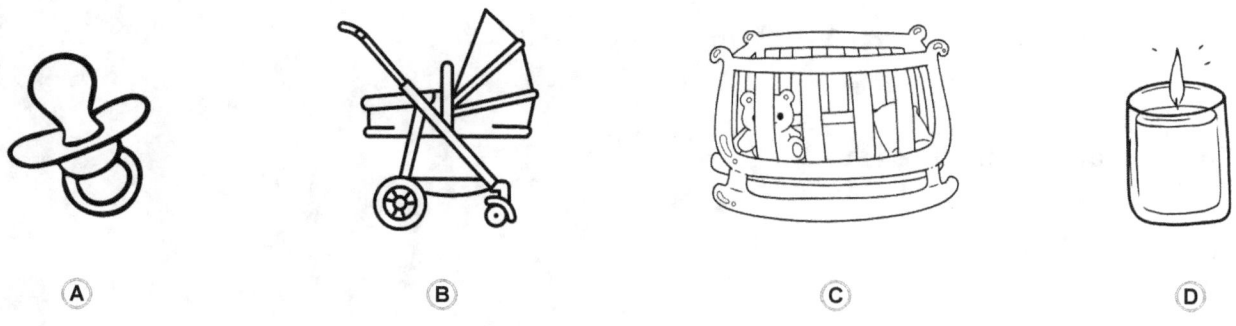

| A | B | C | D |

- End of Practice Test 3. -
- The Answer Key begins on the next page. -

ANSWER KEY FOR PRACTICE TEST 1 (WORKBOOK FORMAT)

Picture Analogies, Practice Test 1

-1. C. A hand goes in a mitten. A foot goes into a sock.

-2. D. To clean your teeth (tooth), you use a toothbrush. To clean your hands (hand), you use soap.

-3. B. A pen and a marker are both used for writing. A microscope and a magnifying glass are both used to make small things appear larger.

-4. B. Dogs are known to carry around bones in their mouths, bury them, and sometimes eat them. A squirrel does the same thing with an acorn.

-5. A. A hammer is a tool used by a carpenter. A fire extinguisher is a tool used by a fireman.

-6. D. A man is the adult, male version of a baby. A male lion is the adult, male version of a lion cub.

-7. D. A chef uses a mixing bowl to create a meal. An artist (a painter) uses a brush and paint to create a painting.

-8. C. A cow produces milk, which is a type of food. A chicken produces eggs, which is a type of food.

-9. A. A farmer rides in a tractor to do his/her job. An astronaut rides in a spaceship to do his/her job.

-10. B. A tadpole goes through metamorphosis and becomes a frog. A caterpillar goes through metamorphosis and becomes a butterfly.

-11. D. The first picture is an open version of the second picture, which is closed. (open mailbox > closed mailbox; open mouth > closed mouth)

-12. C. A bee makes a beehive as its home. A bird makes a nest as its home. (Note that it's not the cage because a cage is made by a person to be the bird's home.)

-13. B. There are 2 similar foods on top (frozen desserts – ice cream and a popsicle) and 2 similar foods on the bottom (fruit – apple and a pear).

-14. D. The number in the left box is the same number of sides that the shape in the right box has.

-15. C. In a coloring book, a crayon is used to add color and complete the design. On an easel, this is done with a paintbrush.

-16. B. A loaf of bread is cut with a knife. A tree is cut with a saw.

Picture Classification, Practice Test 1

-1. D. musical instruments

-2. C. tools

-3. B. things used in writing/drawing/coloring

-4. C. things found in kitchens

-5. D. sweets

-6. C. insects

Picture Classification, Practice Test 1, continued

-7. A. modes of transportation found in the air/sky
-8. B. hot objects
-9. A. shaped like a sphere
-10. D. worn on upper body
-11. C. things that come in pairs
-12. A. animal homes
-13. D. things that are closed
-14. C. different kinds of shells
-15. A. stuffed/toy animals
-16. B. things that hold liquid
-17. B. things that have spots

Sentence Completion, Practice Test 1

-1. C. a firetruck
-2. B. a pillow
-3. D. a winter jacket
-4. A. a saw
-5. D. a chocolate bar
-6. A. grass
-7. C. a pencil
-8. D. a fire
-9. C. a needle and thread
-10. C. a soccer ball
-11. D. a turtle and a lamp
-12. C. a blender
-13. D. a fish
-14. A. a dinosaur
-15. A. a table
-16. D. a fly swatter

ANSWER KEY FOR PRACTICE TEST 2

Picture Analogies, Practice Test 2

-1. C. A car travels on a road. A train travels on train tracks.

-2. D. To consume a drink, you use a straw. To consume ice cream, you use a spoon.

-3. A. The top row has clothing you wear in cold weather. The bottom row has clothing you wear in warm weather. The logic in this one is: similar > similar.

-4. D. The top row has string instruments. The bottom row has large cats. The logic in this one is: similar > similar.

-5. B. Part of a bird is a feather. Part of a tree is a branch.

-6. C. A bird flies in the air. A plane is a vehicle that travels in the air. A duck is an animal that swims in the water. A ship is a vehicle that travels in the water.

-7. C. Full is the opposite of empty. Happy is the opposite of sad.

-8. A. Popcorn is made from corn. Cheese is made from milk.

-9. A. The first picture shows the front (dog, jeep). The second picture shows the back (dog, jeep).

-10. A. A bird eats birdseed. A shark eats fish.

-11. C. The first box shows an animal/person. The second box shows the "hand", a paw of a dog and a hand of a person.

-12. B. Glasses are worn on the eyes. Headphones are worn on the ears.

-13. C. The number of dots in the first box equals the number of wheels on the vehicle in the second box.

-14. D. The first box shows a version of the object as it would be found outside. (A campfire is a version of a fire built outside. A streetlight is a version of a light built outside.) The second box shows a version that is found inside. (A fireplace is a version of fire that's found inside. A lamp is a version of a light found inside.)

-15. A. The top images are things used to measure time. The bottom images are things used to measure distance. The logic in this one is: similar function > similar function.

-16. C. The number of legs the critter has in the first box equals the number of sides of the shape in the second box. In the top box, the number is 6. In the bottom box, the number is 8.

Picture Classification, Practice Test 2

-1. B. warm weather clothes

-2. D. kinds of plants

-3. C. kinds of bags

-4. A. kinds of birds

-5. B. different kinds of things used to house animals/people

-6. A. objects that are open

-7. D. things used to climb

Picture Classification, Practice Test 2, continued

-8. B. cold objects
-9. C. fruit
-10. A. baby animals/babies
-11. B. flat/2D shapes
-12. A. things with stripes
-13. C. worn on head
-14. D. things that have wheels
-15. A. shaped like a cylinder
-16. B. pretend people

Sentence Completion, Practice Test 2

-1. A. a mixing bowl and a whisk
-2. D. a thermometer
-3. A. a scarf
-4. D. a nose
-5. C. binoculars
-6. D. a frog
-7. A. a compass
-8. B. an eagle
-9. C. a flashlight
-10. A. scissors
-11. D. a hose
-12. C. a snake
-13. B. a mirror
-14. B. coffee/tea and a drink with ice
-15. D. an apple (picked from a tree) and grapes (grow on vines)
-16. A. a scale

ANSWER KEY FOR PRACTICE TEST 3

Picture Analogies, Practice Test 3

-1. B. The object in the first box is one slice of the object in the second box.

-2. C. The first box shows a type of weather. The second box shows an activity done in that type of weather. (Snowy weather on top and rainy weather on the bottom.)

-3. D. The first box shows a type of athletic equipment (tennis racket on top and baseball bat on the bottom). The second box shows the type of ball used with that equipment.

-4. A. The first box shows the tool (knife, scissors) used to cut the object in the second box (carrot, paper).

-5. C. The first box shows 1 object. The second box shows a group of those same objects in a container.

-6. A. Clocks and watches are used to tell time. Glasses and cups are used for drinking. The logic in this one is: similar function > similar function.

-7. D. Money is kept in a wallet. Books are kept in a backpack.

-8. A. The first box shows the baby/young version of the animal in the second box.

-9. D. The first box shows the closed version of the object in the second box, which is open.

-10. B. The logic in this one is: similar function > similar function. In the top boxes, the objects are worn on the head. In the bottom boxes, the objects are worn on the feet.

-11. D. Opposites (up vs. down on top; black vs. white on bottom)

-12. C. One object is added to the object in the first box. On top, 1 car becomes 2 cars. On bottom, 2 roses become 3 roses.

-13. B. The objects in the first box are put together to form the object in the second box. Logs are put together to form a log cabin. Pieces of paper are put together to form a notebook.

-14. D. On top, there are sources of water. On bottom, there are sources of light. The logic in this one is: similar function > similar function.

-15. A. The logic here is: time of day > flying animal commonly seen. During the night, bats are seen. During the day, eagles are seen.

-16. B. The first box is a real-life version of the fantasy object in the second box. In the top row is a woman, then a mermaid. In the bottom row is a horse, then a unicorn.

Picture Classification, Practice Test 3

-1. A. things that tell time
-2. C. tools
-3. B. shaped like a cube
-4. A. things that travel underwater
-5. A. vegetables
-6. D. real animals (not stuffed/toy animals)

Picture Classification, Practice Test 3

-7. A. things having to do with the beach
-8. B. things used to measure
-9. C. there is more than one of the same object/there is a group of the same kind of object
-10. A. things used to attach/hold objects together
-11. A. things used for cutting
-12. B. things having to do with 4
-13. D. things that provide light
-14. B. different kinds of shelter/housing for people
-15. D. things requiring electricity to work

Sentence Completion, Practice Test 3

-1. C. a paintbrush
-2. D. a wolf
-3. A. drumsticks
-4. C. a watering can
-5. B. a key
-6. C. a pen
-7. A. a bear
-8. D. a horse
-9. C. half of an apple, a whole pizza, and half of a cookie
-10. B. a camel
-11. B. a book, a pencil, and scissors
-12. C. a turtle
-13. A. a banana
-14. D. a cruise ship
-15. B. a car and a helicopter
-16. D. a candle

Need more practice?

• Help your child **ace the test**!

• Check out **Savant Test Prep**™ books on Amazon®.